Maryville

Maryville
1957 – 2007

JOELLE TAYLOR

BLOOMSBURY POETRY
LONDON · OXFORD · NEW YORK · NEW DELHI · SYDNEY

BLOOSMBURY POETRY
Bloomsbury Publishing Plc
50 Bedford Square, London, WC1B 3DP, UK
Bloomsbury Publishing Ireland Limited,
29 Earlsfort Terrace, Dublin 2, D02 AY28, Ireland

BLOOMSBURY, BLOOMSBURY POETRY and the Diana logo
are trademarks of Bloomsbury Publishing Plc

First published in Great Britain, 2025

Copyright © Joelle Taylor, 2025

Joelle Taylor is identified as the author of this work in accordance with
the Copyright, Designs and Patents Act 1988

This advance reading copy is printed from uncorrected proof pages and is not for resale.
This does not represent the final text and should not be quoted without reference to the final
printed book

All rights reserved. No part of this publication may be: i) reproduced or transmitted in
any form, electronic or mechanical, including photocopying, recording or by means of
any information storage or retrieval system without prior permission in writing from the
publishers; or ii) used or reproduced in any way for the training, development or operation
of artificial intelligence (AI) technologies, including generative AI technologies. The rights
holders expressly reserve this publication from the text and data mining exception as per
Article 4(3) of the Digital Single Market Directive (EU) 2019/790

Bloomsbury Publishing Plc does not have any control over, or responsibility for, any third-
party websites referred to in this book. All internet addresses given in this book were correct
at the time of going to press. The author and publisher regret any inconvenience caused if
addresses have changed or sites have ceased to exist,
but can accept no responsibility for any such changes

A catalogue record for this book is available from the British Library

ISBN: HB: 978-1-5266-8048-8;
eBook: 978-1-5266-8052-5 ; ePDF: 978-1-5266-8049-5

2 4 6 8 10 9 7 5 3 1

Typeset by Laura Jones-Rivera
Printed and bound in Great Britain by
CPI Group (UK) Ltd, Croydon CR0 4YY

To find out more about our authors and books
visit www.bloomsbury.com and sign up for our newsletters
For product-safety-related questions contact productsafety@bloomsbury.com

for wrong walking women

Contents

Foreword — 1
Characters — 5

EPISODE ONE, SEASON ONE: 1957-1967
a silence filled with dancing

MISE-EN-SCÈNE: Establishing Shot	9
Jack Catch: The House of Detention	12
A Murmuration of Starlings: summarise the trial of young Jack	14
Jack Catch: My Body an Ambush	15
Jack Catch: The Laundry Room	16
Ruby: The Mentor	18
MISE-EN-SCÈNE: Dudizile	19
Dudizile: Conversion Therapy	21
Dudizile: Homo Sweet Homo	22
Dudizile: The Family Tailor	25
Dudizile: pin the pieces together to make a pattern	27
MISE-EN-SCÈNE: Valentine	30
Valentine: The Brothers Grin	32
Valentine: Tinkering Beneath Bonnets	34
MISE-EN-SCÈNE: A Flock of Startled Things Tells the Story of ANGEL	36
Angel: Möbius Fist	38
Angel: Boy-Boys	39
Jack Catch: King Jack	40
MISE-EN-SCÈNE: Jack Catch	42
Valentine: Pride	44
Angel: An Invitation to Attend the Ball	46
Maryville: A Word We Do Not Know	47
MISE-EN-SCÈNE: Maryville 1957	48
Soho: Hi Femme	51
Dudizile: Mr Ben	53

EPISODE TWO, SEASON ONE: 1977-1987
rebels with a clause

MISE-EN-SCÈNE: 1977-1987	59
Ruby: The Door	61
MISE-EN-SCÈNE: Thank You Strange Lady	62
Soho: A Flock of Femmes Alight a Field	63
The Bois: Penetration is Oppression	65
Jack Catch: 2 x 20	68
Angel: Shadow Boxing	69
The Bois: Cock Sonnets	70
Soho: The Flight of the Femmes	73
Jack Catch: Moon Over Charing Cross Road	75
MISE-EN-SCÈNE: Valentine Finds Railton Road	76
Valentine: On Railton Road	78
Angel: Rapture	80
MISE-EN-SCÈNE: London Fields: The Lesbians Are Coming	82
Family: The Bent Resistance Attends a Stop the Clause Meeting	84
Soho: Another Nail on the Cross at Calvary	86
Library Footage	89
MISE-EN-SCÈNE: It Says It's A Girl	91
Valentine: Brixton Riots	93
MISE-EN-SCÈNE: A Maryville Christmas	96
MISE-EN-SCÈNE: Angel	99
Angel: The Death of God	101
Family: Split / Screen	102
MISE-EN-SCÈNE: Maryville Celeste	107
MISE-EN-SCÈNE: Nothing Nothing Nothing	109
MISE-EN-SCÈNE: Jack & Soho	110
MISE-EN-SCÈNE: Funeral for A Friend	113

EPISODE THREE, SEASON ONE 1997-2007
dust kings. tough kids

MISE-EN-SCÈNE 1997-2007	121
Coin Slot	123
Soho: Vespertine	124
The Bois: Halo	125
Dudizile: Quipu	126
Soho: The Femme Telegraph	128
MISE-EN-SCÈNE: Everyone Is Still Alive	129
The Bois: The O God	131
MISE-EN-SCÈNE: Snow Globes	132
all of the ghosts. all of them.	133
dust kings. tough kids. i-xv	134
Jack Catch: Old Jack Takes a Long Walk Back to the Beginning	149
Old Bois: 2007	151
Old Bois: Prelude	158
Old Bois: The Door	162
Old Bois: The World Was Ending & It Was Time to Dance	163
Old Bois: Homecoming	165
MISE-EN-SCÈNE: O Maryville O	167
End Notes	*170*
Glossary of Dyke Slang	*172*
Glossary of Film Vocabulary	*173*
Cultural References	*174*
Acknowledgements	*177*

Courage is not defined by those who fought and did not fall, but by those who fought, fell, and rose again.

– Adrienne Rich

FOREWORD

In this book we remember the journey and honour the road.

Maryville follows the lives of the four butch dyke friends first introduced in *C+NTO & Othered Poems* and reimagines them entering The Maryville bar in 1957, remaining there until 2007. This 50-year time span covers a significant period in the evolution of both LGBT rights and the women's liberation movement in the UK, an essential backdrop to the poetry of this book. I return to the same people in the same space; sometimes we cannot escape the stories that write us.

Maryville is a poetry collection in the shape of a television series, using the language of film to steer a way into each poem, to focus, and pull out into the wide-angle narrative. It is a visual poem because I want you to see us. I want us to see ourselves. I want us to recognise that our exclusion from the mainstream was the very thing that gave us the space to rethink the potentiality of our lives. The dyke bar was a space of radical reinvention of the self, a space where community ruptured into friendships and bar fights, where politics was ingrained on each knuckle.

This was a decision I made not just in terms of honouring the cinema of poetry but because I have never seen myself or my distinct community accurately reflected on mainstream television. Writing about representation of lesbians Claudia Cahalane of *The Guardian*[i] cited a study of BBC output 'which found that lesbians contributed to just two minutes of programming from a randomly selected 39 hours of broadcasts'.

With this collection I wanted to create a visual record of who we are, what we have endured and how we turned suffering into a well-cut suit, a language of our own. It is about the joy of meeting, and the grief at the heart of love. I wanted to give us an extra two minutes.

Each *Mise-En-Scène* poem has a soundtrack – for the most part popular gay anthems from the specific time written about. Play them as you read. Step into the scene.

The queered crown of sonnets, *Dust Kings. Tough Kids*, references butch lesbians who have been murdered for their appearance and sexuality, for the fact of their female dissidence. Seventy-six countries currently criminalise sex between people of the same sex[ii] and we know that violence against lesbians, especially the masculine presenting, is on the rise. The United Nations in Latin America reports increasing violence and murder enacted against lesbians, with Brazil reporting the highest rates, followed by Mexico. In South Africa there are numerous accounts of 'corrective rape' meted against butch lesbians – with studies suggesting 25 per cent (a conservative figure) of lesbians having experienced sexual violence. Similar 'corrective' violence is perpetrated in Chile's Red Zone. Amnesty International also notes high levels of violence against lesbians or suspected lesbians across Middle Eastern countries, along with Pakistan and India. Nearly one third of lesbian women in Zimbabwe, Botswana, Namibia and South Africa have reported experiences of sexual violence[iii].

Stop Violence Against Women noted: 'Women who do not conform to societal expectations of sexuality and gender presentation are at heightened risk of violence based on their sexuality or gender identity.'[iv] Erin Kilbride of Human Rights Watch wrote in the report *This Is Why We Became Activists* (2023)[v] that homophobia toward masculine-presenting women means that butch lesbians face a lifetime of social discrimination, economic marginalisation, overrepresentation in the prison system, workplace harassment and consistent psychological abuse. In some countries this is supported by security forces who target those women for sexual and physical violence. 'There is clearly a kind of rage from men and from security forces based on our research that is incited by women who dare to take up masculine space in the world – space that cisgender men think belongs to them alone', said Kilbride.

Despite this, support for the lesbian community is underfunded globally even within LGBT+ organisations. This is due in part to the need to directly address laws that discriminate against gay men and trans people, but it has led to a misperception that lesbians – especially the gender non-conforming – are not in immediate danger. The reality is that homophobia is compounded by misogyny – then by classism and racism – to create a perfect storm of silence.

The struggle of lesbians intersects with the struggles of women globally. I have previously written of the Purge in Chechnya, how lesbians and gay men (specifically) are targeted by the security forces and subjected to extreme state violence. The Rainbow Railroad in Russia works to extract those in danger and funnel them to safe countries. While gay men can leave their houses independently and work in other territories, thereby making it easier to extract them, rescuing lesbians is extremely difficult in a culture that does not allow women independence from male authority. She cannot travel alone, leave the house alone, secure employment, attend higher education or make decisions without consulting male family members. We have all witnessed the horrors afflicting the women of Afghanistan under Taliban rule; how should we help those lesbians?

While this collection is set in London, on the shelves behind the Maryville bar are a thousand snow globes. Inside each is a different bar (an imaginative space, a parenthesis) in a different country, within which similar epics of intimacy and expansion are played out. For the butch dyke, the difference between politic and body are indistinguishable.

The lesbian is both invisible and hyper-visible in the same moment. Invisible to culture and politics, but all too apparent to those who wish us harm.

CHARACTERS

The Maryville
An old breathless bar at the end of an abandoned alleyway in East London. She is gaudy, overstated, discrete & defiant. She is a nation of exiles and outcasts. She remembers everything, says nothing.

Jack Catch
Jack Catch is the butch bartender at The Maryville bar. We meet her as a young teen in HMP Martyrs Hill and follow her for 50 years as she navigates the world and carves out a space for herself and other women like her. Taciturn, shy, & with permeating sadness, she is the quintessential butch.

Dudizile
Jack's best friend. Dudizile is an unofficial LGBT refugee from South Africa, escaping corrective rape in her hometown to find a kind of freedom in Elephant & Castle, London. She is a tailor who had dreamed of becoming a doctor.

Valentine
A car mechanic and the founder of a dyke motorbike gang, she is one of the four butches/ studs. A leather dyke, a feminist, and a Black Panther, Valentine is the heartthrob of the book.

Angel
A young boi, determined to become a boxer at her local ring

where she works as a short order cook in the attached all-night cafe. She is wide-eyed and violent, gentle and addicted. She is mothered by her three friends.

Soho
King femme, & Jack's girlfriend. She is a pivotal character, the soul of the bar, more metaphor than flesh. She is The Meta-Femme. She is The Maryville.

The Femmes
Women who perform the idea of Woman, as gender non-conforming as the butches. Hard to spot on the street, impossible to miss in the bar. Part of the butch-femme dynamic.

Ruby
The bouncer on the door of The Maryville, & Jack's mentor in prison. Ruby is an old school butch whose life purpose is to protect the door at The Maryville, & all the women inside.

Boy-Boys
A group of white men who stand outside The Maryville bar for 50 years, trying to get in and harassing women as they leave. Like the butches, they first appear outside the Maryville in the late 1950s and age alongside the four friends.

Valentine's Brothers
Melvyn and Costcutter. They are both black men in their early 30s in the late 1950s who have inherited their father's mechanic's garage. The teach their little sister how to work engines. They teach her how to be loved.

EPISODE ONE, SEASON ONE

1957 – 1967

a silence filled with dancing

MISE-EN-SCÈNE

The Sky Above HMP Martyrs Hill
1957

|| WIDE SHOT: AN ENGLISH MORNING, AUTUMN. A STRIPTEASE OF TREES FLASH THE WIND ||

An industrial sky, over-washed & badly hung. The sun considers its nails as clouds gather like teenagers. As though scripted, a brown bird strays into shot, cursor across a grey screensaver, & aims directly into the centre of the camera lens. It perches on the rim for a moment, as though about to feed. Reflected in the bird's eyes is a sign the colour of obedience.

|| CUT TO EXTREME CLOSE-UP OF EYES: *CORRECTIVE TRAINING. HMP MARTYRS HILL* ||

The brown bird launches into the exultant nothing.

|| CUT TO POV THE BROWN BIRD, AERIAL SHOT ||

From above the prison is under-written, over-dressed & short of breath. From this height the bird thinks the panopticon looks like a concrete web – a living thing that catches living things to store for later, when the winter comes. In this way, she thinks, all the tiny women in their tiny cells are seeds in husks. She wonders what might grow from them. She dives toward the metal sign.

|| SNAP FADE WIDE SHOT ||

The bird balances on the edge of the sign. When it sings, a chorus of male voices elbow out:

> *'I imagine [she] would have preferred
> to have been raped by a man'*[vi]

|| POV THE BIRD, TRACKING SHOT ||

The bird flies between the prison gates, past sleep-thickened guards, through locked keyholes and on and on, beyond free flow, beyond the rec room, beyond huddled Formica tables, until she reaches the eye of the web. She rests for a moment on the peak of a warden's cap. She peers along the linoleum throat of a corridor that never sings, tilting her head to sip at the idea of iron stairs, iron bannisters, the iron air, the iron wind, a wall that wishes it were elsewhere, a floor that does not believe the foot.

At the end of the corridor a door gasps, once, then bursts open to reveal a young woman stood vigil beside a single bed. She stares at the ground as though it were a love letter.

JACK CATCH

The House of Detention

young Jack interprets
the air   taps her teeth
to the click of clockwork
women wound & pointed
their heels tiny cogs
Jack is confined
to her body
her keyhole turned
stoppered handcuffed
to the bars
of her rib cage
reformed the shape
of girl

                                        Jack in a box

the factory
of femininity
blinks cinches
its corsetry
the floors fizz
into circuit boards
& the skirting boards
curtsy as the governor
thrills through
the walls are ideas
& the fences
barbed wire XX
it is here

women are mended
rebuilt in the image
of their fathers
here that women
are pieced together
beneath the guard's
mechanical eye
even Jack's blood cells
have guards   she wonders
who else is lost
in the fingerprint
labyrinth   if there are other
notwomen here   incarcerated
in dresses cut from the skin
of teeth   making the women
sacks   containing women.

JACK TURNS TOWARD THE BARRED WINDOW. THROUGH ITS IRON EYELASHES SHE WATCHES A MURMURATION OF STARLINGS CONGREGATING. THEY BOW THEIR HEADS & BEGIN

A MURMURATION OF STARLINGS

summarise the trial of young Jack

                              starlings
                    conjure a face   kid girl   it hangs
            a wet photograph   knitting wind   before it
               dissolves into the outline of a father   backing out of the frame
                          there and not there
& as he locks the door between us   the keyhole melts into the shape of two girls
       kissing   the meeting of lips   a breath starling   fallen from flock
           how it forgets   the ground   how it does not understand
                          the borders in air   [   ]
         diving into   the wide & alive   stupid with body   beyond the hearing
of congregation
                   its song   a club aria   disco opera   the trill
                    of washing up & quiet nights in   but then the starlings
                        plummet into a fist
                      black as tabloid ink
     & each starling has its own role here   this one: the fury of a passerby
           this one: an inarticulate mother   tripping over obscenity
                          this one: the obscenity
        this one: a tick of police   other birds play a judicial shadow   as
                 that divides   the two girls
                       another: a public unpeeling
         while still more unite to play the van   that takes a blunt faced girl away
                another: the window the girl-faced girl leans against
                     the murmuration stills
                     tea leaves awaiting water
                    before collapsing into a court order
                          each bird calligraphy   then
                                      signature   then
                                     stamp
                                    until the
                                    murmur
                                    ation is
                                     a gavel   slowly
                                    descend
                                     ing bring
                                     ing the
                                      night
                                       with
                                        it.

JACK

My Body an Ambush

Jack is framed / within the cell door keyhole / making her a woman imprisoned / in the body of a woman / a sand timer / she is falling through her own hands / it is true / the crime is the punishment / young jack / holding girls who mistook her for themselves / falling in love like others fall in front of trains / when Elizabeth denied her / three times / she transmuted a kiss under a name / to a wrought iron crucifix / curtsying to men / cassocked as crows / swore Jack was a boy / a charming violence / that she kept her clothes on beneath her skin / that the night is unnatural / that Jack was a fraudster / interloper / thief of the quiet places / thirty pieces of fucking / & now the sun is locked in a metal box / shown to the women / once a day / if you are good / you can hold it / if you are bad / you can hold it / & Jack lays still / listening to night talk / preen the wing / the animal of their mouths / searching for their young / afraid of the soft predator / concealed in the bushes / the rustle of leaving.

The Laundry Room

|| WIDE ANGLE: CHEWING OF WASHING MACHINES. GASP OF STEAM PRESS. A SMUDGE OF ROOM. JACK WITH BACK TURNED TO US, IS FEEDING THE MOUTHS OF WASHING MACHINES AS IF THEY ARE THE CHILDREN OF STARLINGS ||

Jack washes her mother first / draping her gently over the iron ribs of a radiator / then turns to her father / unsure of how to remove the stain / that has become him / can alcohol remove alcohol? / how to dissolve these bonds / she mixes her neighbours together in the same load / ignores the banging drum / the orange whistles & pipes / the whole band / she bleaches her classmates on boil / a rebirth in amniotic ammonia / then mangles newspapers & magazines / punching them into the howling belly of the machine / firing them on permanent press / (yes there is irony / even here) / steam rises across the room / gathering like the ghosts of gossips / over garden walls / as Jack's clothes evaporate to join them / in narrating her / & now o God / she is naked / in the laundry room / on the high street / in court / & everything is gone / look at it all / gone / just –

A CHORUS OF GOSSIPING STEAM WATCHES AS JACK LETS THE UNWASHED LAUNDRY FALL AROUND HER LIKE BIRDS SHOT FROM PURE SKIES & SLIPS TO HER KNEES. THE STARLING CHILDREN GAPE.

THE STEAM SOLIDIFIES INTO THE FORM OF RUBY, HOLDING DIRTY BED SHEETS BY THEIR NECKS. SHE

RELEASES THEM & PLUCKS A COMB FROM HER BACK POCKET, WHICH SHE DRAWS THROUGH HER SILVER BRYLCREAMED QUIFF. THE LINES ON HER FACE BECOME POETRY, OVERWRITTEN. AFTER A MOMENT, RUBY PLACES A HEAVY HAND ON JACK'S SHOULDER, WHO TURNS & SEES HERSELF FOR THE FIRST TIME.

SLOW FADE TO STEAM WHITE.

RUBY

The Mentor

Born from a sailor's knot / lips a sealed envelope / silvershave & soft belly / Ruby squats her body as though it were tenement / filled with family / an ashtray overflowing / a shout up the stairwell / her thick white arms / the width of belief / strong, unrelenting / the great butch mother / her breasts a desk toy / her face a club comedian / easy to draw / her mouth a steam iron / star sign, amphetamine / a rubbed blue anchor under her wristwatch / her fists come / in dribs & drabs / & she hangs them to dry alongside prison issue uniforms / while her femme fixes her makeup / in the shine of her boots / when Ruby washes clothes / they stay clean / she folds each sheet / as though it were a returned love letter / marks her initial on the underside / so all the girls know / who they will be sleeping with tonight.

RUBY TAKES JACK BY THE HAND & SEATS HER ON A STACK OF LAUNDERED SHEETS. SHE DOES NOT LOOK AT JACK BUT ROLLS THEM BOTH SKINNY CIGARETTES. SHE FLICKS HER ZIPPO ON HER OUTER THIGH & LIGHTS THEM.

MISE-EN-SCÈNE

Dudizile

SOUNDTRACK: *Pata Pata,* Miriam Makeba

GRAINY BLACK & WHITE SUPER 8 FILM, HANDHELD

EXTERIOR, NOON. SOPHIATOWN, JOHANNESBURG – SOUTH AFRICA 1957

|| EXTREME CRANE SHOT: A THIN LINE OF MEN CHASE A YOUNG BOI THROUGH AN INTENSTINAL CITYSCAPE ||

// jackrollers[vii] whistle & whoop / costume lions / roars handed down from big brothers / too baggy for their mouths / they take chase as though it were communion / & when they catch her / there will be a parade / there will be a great unlearning / Dudizile is a solution / in need of a problem / a dress blue-pencilled to the wrong pattern / a suit cut from rumours / her shoes know they are leaving / have known for years/ her breath already in England / she runs / out of her clothes / beyond her body / & keeps running / she will collect herself later / have it air mailed / but now the dust corrects her / the open eye of the sky is a door / the air is packing its bags / behind her / the chase becomes a queue: / the boys at the back of the class / the father of her best friend / a third cousin / the man from the bakery / her therapist / her mother's minister / a pastor / god / / the girl she winked at / if she had looked back / she might have seen herself / chasing her too / & now she is running out of country / but Dudz is a narrow side street / knows how to twist & sudden / she runs along dual carriageways / weaving between traffic / & runs on to a bus that becomes a train carriage/ that she runs the length of / until it reaches an airport that she runs into / flashing her chest at security / & onto a plane / & keeps on running / past business class / through economy / along the centre aisle / & out the back door onto a dark London pavement / wept by a chilled rain / that collapses to its knees in welcome / as she runs onto a quiet Victorian terrace street / toward the slow opening of a blue door //

FADE TO FULL COLOUR AS WE APPROACH THE DOOR. AN OLDER WOMAN IS ILLUMINATED IN IT, WEARING A MATCHING MAXI DRESS & HEAD SCARF. DUDIZILE CROSSES HER ARMS OVER HER CHEST, CLOSES HER EYES, & FALLS BACKWARD INTO THE HOUSE.

DUDIZILE

Conversion Therapy

her family / a ministry of dogs / well trained & sullen / straight-back around the dining table / balance glossy brochures in their mouths / she is shown a photograph of a beautiful woman / & electrocuted / feels a wet nose / & is injected with self-doubt / a rising tide of sick & flinch / when she sees a female / her hands escape & hide behind her / when she thinks of love / she thinks of death / she wonders / what she will be converted into / student accommodation / an unexpected mezzanine / a holiday home on the edge of a grin / it's ok / no / it's ok / sit / they throw the treatment / but she will not fetch / just runs with it / wriggling between her teeth / & converts it into a plane ticket.

Homo Sweet Homo

& now she sits
centre stage
of a tight-lipped
settee flanked
by three voluminous
aunties opposed
by sad uncles
on low seating
they offer a buffet
of hello small things
as their tongues unroll
into welcome mats
with colonial font
they have trussed
her in a torniquet
dress flower on top
relax they smile
eat cake a radio
resumes its catechism
uncles mark newspapers
with blunt pencils
she grins
like a garden gate
in a high wind
noting a distinct
& British chill
frost the carpet
creep up the queen
anne legs

spreading
snowflakes
like
    anti
        macassar

|| DOLLY SHOT: WE FOLLOW DUDIZILE & HER NEW FAMILY ACROSS LONDON TO A SMALL TAILOR'S IN ELEPHANT & CASTLE. INSIDE, IT IS NARROW DARK ||

The Family Tailor

the walls are laddered
with shelves storing
men from boyhood
to evensong, a trill
of masculinity
starched upper
lips arranged
in order of grit
a clench of white
collars, an arrest
of white cuffs
fabric swatches
catalogue
gesture, place
& discernment
while suits
in the act of
birth hang
from umbilical
ropes dancing
in the late
afternoon solemn
buttons blink
& a mannequin
clears its throat of
leaving, air kissing
the shop, offering
blue chalk
tailor's tape

French curve
& an infinity
of fathers
waiting
in the mirror.

pin the pieces together according to the pattern

i

first, they dress
her as themselves
Cousin John holds out
a hole for her to climb into
& it fits her perfectly
perhaps he will need to
let it out a little around
the thought, but not yet.
she introduces herself
to the speculative mirror
wonders how it knows
she is there
if it watches her leave.

ii

grief is an aftershave.

iii

at the cutting desk
they trace chalk lines
around the living
crooken and straighten
hem their frayed tongues
birdseye mohair tweed
gaberdine twill

hopsack flannel
pinstripe houndstooth
neck base to thumb knuckle
behold the measure of a man.
Dudizile holds the fabric
as if it were her mother.

iv

today she will make a skin:
a suit sewn from identity papers
a plane ticket pocket square
she lays the pattern flat
hands in the air
a curling map
of Johannesburg
& remembers the run
to keep up with her body
as she pins the blood her
lips a tacking stitch.

v

Dudizile is mannequin
stood twilight
in the shop, flickering
in a shapeshifting suit
quiet as men
catching buses to funerals
dressed in dusk
she adjusts each white cuff
measures one half inch precisely

tucks her ruler
inside left pocket
shines a shoe on the back of her calf
& waits
hands landing softly in front
like long haul
like prayer.

MISE-EN-SCÈNE

Valentine

SOUNDTRACK: *Pretty Woman, Roy Orbison*

|| POV CAR. WALNUT DASHBOARD. WHITE STEERING WHEEL. SKY LIKE A USED OIL FILTER ||

WE DRIVE THROUGH OLD RAILWAY ARCHES TOWARDS A GRIMY MECHANIC SHOP. WE PASS A BLACK MAN, EARLY 30s, AS WE DRIVE IN. HE WAVES AS THOUGH FLICKING A CRUMB FROM HIS SHIRT. THE CAR PARKS. THE DRIVER'S DOOR OPENS.

OIL BOTTLES, ANTI FREEZE, VARIOUS WRENCHES, SCREWDRIVERS & PLIERS. CABLES SPOOLED IN LEMNISCATE. A SPOTLIGHT OF DIRTY SUN WANDERS THROUGH THE DOOR & RESTS BY A PAIR OF BOOTED FEET STICKING OUT FROM UNDER A CAR HELD UP BY JACKS.

|| CLOSE-UP OF: BOOTS. WELL-WORN & SCRUPULOUS, DUBBIN RUBBED & METHODICAL. THEY SHOOT TOWARD US ||

VALENTINE, A YOUNG BLACK BOI WITH POMADED HAIR, PUSHES OUT FROM BENEATH THE CAR. SHE IS A THRILL IN SEARCH OF A FACE. ABOVE HER IS A TWIN SET WOMAN WITH A BOUFFANT & CALF SKIN GLOVES. SHE PASSES A SMALL CARD TO VALENTINE WHO READS & GRINS. HER LAUGHTER IS A CAR STARTING ON A COLD WET DAY.

|| CAMERA SLOWLY ZOOMS INTO ONE OF VALENTINE'S EYES UNTIL THE PUPIL TAKES UP THE WHOLE OF THE FRAME. IN IT ARE TWO MEN WITH SMILES LIKE WASHING LINES. VALENTINE'S CLOTHES HANG FROM THEM. ONE IS COOKING DINNER LIKE HE IS PLAYING RECORDS, & THE OTHER TICKING OFF FOOTBALL TEAMS FOR THE POOL THAT EVENING. THEY ARE MELVYN & COSTCUTTER, VALENTINE'S BROTHERS & LOCUS PARENTI ||

The Brothers Grin

While Valentine
builds her motorbike
in the back yard
from the offcuts
of conversations
her brothers quietly
build her, each a
motherless sun,
elder, definite,
muscles like brake
cables , watching
her grow into the
shape
of a well-oiled thing
how happy she is
to fall,
this dust king
this tough kid
optimum engine
each riding shotgun
wing men for wrong
women, her brothers
have all the body
work she needs
& they hold her
like a clockwork
hummingbird
in their palms
show her the drown

of the sky, how deep
it is, how fragile
knowing all it takes
is one bad driver
for the road to return
to its source.

Tinkering Beneath Bonnets

the metaphor here
is not worth writing
(is beneath the poem)
how the under carriage
is a reproductive system
how the car is pregnant with
road, how Valentine lies
under the unsure chassis
making promises
she has no intention
of keeping, fingers
slick with the wet dark
looking deep into the O
of the engine, the wonder
of absence, the insistent
hello, Valentine
considers whether this model
is convertible
who exactly it is registered
to, whether it would like
a full service, a dinner perhaps
some cinema to liven
this dual carriageway
of a day. Valentine tests
the suspension
holds out her
hand for a spanner
lets the car roll its r's
the window wipers arch

when she pulls it back
there is a card in her palm
a name printed centrally
& *Maryville* scrawled
in a skid of lipstick
on the inverse.
In the underdark
the lettering looks
like tyre tracks
leaving the road.

MISE-EN-SCÈNE

A Flock of Startled Things Tell the Story of ANGEL

SOUNDTRACK: *Young Blood,* The Coasters

EXTERIOR, EARLY MORNING. SPRING.

|| BIRDS EYE VIEW WIDE ANGLE ||

A crowd gathers around the shape of a girl dressed like a boy. ANGEL lies face up on the floor, draped in spit, her red cheeks blooming into a Mother's Day present. Boy-boys stare down at her as if she is a red puzzle.

|| BIRDS EYE VIEW ZOOM OUT ||

From above the crowd looks like spilled ink. It pulses three times then dilates, fanning out across wasteland, beyond the chicken shop & boarded up pawn shop. It shudders then solidifies into thick font. The crowd quickly types across the playing field and walkways:

|| TRACKING SHOT AS SENTENCES APPEAR ACROSS THE RINSE ESTATE FORMING A TELEGRAM ||

SIRS -

Angel works shy & shadow alone in the all night café Roman Road boxing ring where the windows have glaucoma but cannot get an appointment (STOP) From the sink she watches the corner boys bolo from The Rinse dance into the ring (STOP) flashy & wide   more pride than punch more punch than think feint & salvo jab & clinch (STOP) Their bare chests locked & buried we are redeemed through the letting   through ichor & gold (STOP) See them spit in the boxing ring of their blood each perfect O+ aa boxer wrapping a fist (STOP) She looks down to see her marigolds shapeshift to boxing gloves feels her bicep stand up & shout (STOP) a tough kid someone's sister (STOP) the Lords of Nothing Much shake   her between their teeth like a fetish a returning doll in a horror film leaving her lain in the body of a girl her blood running to her neighbours who turn to face her their eyes small circles with men dancing inside (ST

ANGEL

Möbius Fist

Rinse Estate / the shape of a broken nose / black & white brutalism / something Scorsese / a concrete kiss / a corridor that leads to a corridor / that leads to a girl being beaten into the shape of girl / but still Angel rises / her fists / a flock of startled birds / editing the grey skies / even the air is hungry around here / when she climbs into the boxing ring / she is standing on the head of a map pin / how an O is also a returned wedding ring / is a neighbour's eye / is also the mark left by a coffee cup / in an all-night café / & now Angel unravels her fists / into Möbius strips / & now film negatives / each frame / a moment in her rethinking: the circle of men / the spittle confetti / the press ups above some girl / pull ups from lisping door frames / a girl climbing into a dress & disappearing / the kind of tiger / who escapes the bars across her body / knowing her bruises are breadcrumbs / & she just needs to follow them / & maybe at the end of the path of wounds / she will find / a body that can take a fist / & turn it into a bunch of flowers.

Boy-Boys

|| OVER SHOULDER SHOT OF ANGEL NAVIGATING THE RINSE ESTATE, SHOULDERS RAISED LIKE RIFLES, HEAD TUNNELING AN ESCAPE ROUTE INTO THE EARLY MORNING AIR. THE CAMERA GLANCES AT A BLOCK OF FLATS, WHOSE LIT WINDOWS SEMPAHORE A RESIGNED 'SOS' ||

the boy-boys edit the pavement / narrating their world into being / their words, seeds / from which cities grow / sullen gatherings exit their stadium mouths / honourable pillages / sky scrapers shoot up around them / (ill-timed erections) / & in each building / another boy-boy / & another / each at their saddening windows / shouting into the abandoned above / peering through bead curtains of sweat / at women entering the bar alone / & exiting as a chorus line / stroking the why at the centre of them / feeding the fuck / the tilt & the swagger / in this way / they are archetypal time / pink calendars / each member / a spoke in a sun dial / casting its shadow across Maryville / the same boy-boys / every Friday night in summer / gathering like alley flies / around the door / corner boys with grins like cul-de-sacs / Angel knows them all / they are her brothers / gods of the underpass / prince piss stain / circling manhood like kicked dogs / growing from the knuckle outward / an altar boy / uncurling.

JACK

King Jack

|| CAMERA DOLLIES ALONG SERPENTINE GREY CORRIDORS PAUSING TO OPEN BARRED METAL GATES, FOLLOWING JACK AS SHE IS DRAGGED BY GUARDS TOWARD A SMALL METAL DOOR. A SIGN READS 'CORRECTION'. SHE IS BEING INTERRED IN THE STRIPviii AS A REMINDER OF HOW SMALL HER BODY IS. SHE IS NOT SHOUTING ||

THE DOOR OPENS & JACK IS EATEN BY THE ROOM.

Jack's hair grows like escaping women / each follicle / tunneling through her scalp / toward the endless bright / she imagines her hair is leaving her too / is migrant somehow / is seeing someone else perhaps / Ruby tuts / palms her a pair of scissors / *keep it dapper, king* / she whispers / *keep it king* / & Jack cuts her hair into a crown / & now she is the gutter prince / padlocked into a dress / & stored in The Strip / where women are dissolved into yes / but Ruby was right / now Jack rules her own face / this kingdom of bones / this endless forget / sitting cross legged / on an invertebrate throne / in a room without windows / listening to the tick of heels along corridors / the theme tune of keys / she stares at the keyhole / *how woman*, she thinks / unsure if she is locked in one / or standing outside / a bunch of keys / wilting in her hand.

JACK REMAINS CROSS LEGGED ON THE FLOOR, A BARE MATTRESS BESIDE HER. THERE IS A SMILE SOMEWHERE TO THE SIDE OF HER.

SLOW CAMERA FADE TO BLACK, LEAVING JACK'S UNBLINKING EYES ILLUMINATED IN THE DARK.

MISE-EN-SCÈNE

Release Day

SOUNDTRACK: *Walking After Midnight,* Patsy Cline

EXTERIOR, HMP MARTYRS HILL:

THE PRISON GATES OPEN & A GRINNING RUBY IS RELEASED BACK IN TO THE WILD. SHE BREAKS INTO THE DAY, STRIDING INTO SHOT. THE DOOR SLAMS. AFTER A FEW MOMENTS IT TENTATIVELY OPENS AGAIN TO REVEAL JACK, HER EYES FIXED ON SOMETHING OUT OF FRAME, HER BODY THE SOFT BEFORE FLINCH.

|| TRACKING SHOT: RUBY WEARS THE PRISON IN HER PIN STRIPE SUIT, HER CLOTHES MORE IDEA THAN FABRIC. JACK THINKS THAT RUBY LOOKS LIKE A BULLET IMAGINES IT DOES. JACK TRAILS RUBY ACROSS LONDON UNTIL SHE REACHES A SIDE STREET IN A SIDEWAYS PART OF TOWN. AT THE BORDER, EXILED FROM THE OTHER BUILDINGS, IS A BAR, ITS BACK TURNED TOWARD US, ITS WINDOWS GLAUCOMIC, ITS PINK NEON SIGN FLASH AS UNCLES. IT IS THE KIND OF BAR THAT COMES HOME LATE WEARING SOMEONE ELSE'S JACKET ||

EXTERIOR, MARYVILLE BAR

|| CLOSE-UP: THE SIGN COUGHS *MARYVILLE* THEN COVERS ITS MOUTH ||

JACK HANGS BACK AND WATCHES AS RUBY STRAIGHTENS HER OVERCOAT. SHE KNOCKS ON THE DOOR, THE SOUND ECHOING JACK'S HEARTBEAT. MARYVILLE WINKS AND OPENS HER RED LEGS. RUBY ENTERS, LEAVING THE DOOR SLIGHTLY PARTED. THERE IS SOMETHING ALIVE WITHIN.

|| RACK SHOT: A GIGGLE OF BOY-BOYS STANDS IN THE STREET DUSK SCUFFING A SMOKE, THEIR EYES APERTURES. PULL FOCUS. DILATE. ZOOM ||

THE SHARED GHOST OF THEIR CIGARETTE FOLLOWS JACK INTO THE BAR. SLOW FADE TO BLACK. VOICE OVER: AMBIENT NATTER AND THRILL.

VALENTINE

Pride

SOUNDTRACK: *Putting on the Style,* Lonnie Donegan

|| WIDE CAMERA ANGLE OF VALENTINE'S LIVING ROOM. IT IS A WARM ROOM, UNTIDY BUT LOVED. ANTI MACASSARS STAINED WITH ENGINE OIL ARE DRAPED OVER THE BACKS OF THE CHAIRS. A GAS FIRE GRITS ITS TEETH ||

VALENTINE STANDS BEFORE HER ELDER BROTHERS WHO HAVE INTERROGATED THEIR WARDROBES FOR A SHIRT & TIE FOR HER TO WEAR WITH HER FORMAL SLACKS. THEY HOLD UP THEIR OFFERINGS LIKE FISH AT MARKET & SHE CHOOSES A POLO SHIRT THE COLOUR OF REVOLT. ONE BROTHER IRONS HER HAIR WHILE ANOTHER RUBS VASELINE INTO HER FACE, ARMS, KNEES. THEY KNEAD HER INTO HANDSOME. WHEN FINISHED THEY PRESS A TEN SHILLING NOTE INTO HER PALM. SHE CLOSES HER FINGERS & LAUGHS.

|| SLOW CROSS FADE TO VALENTINE OVER SHOULDER SHOT READING THE SIGN FOR *'MARYVILLE'*. SHE PUSHES OPEN THE DOOR TO A BRIGHT CIRCUS & WALKS FORWARD STILL LAUGHING, HAIR POMADED IN PETROL, ONE ARM SLUNG ACROSS THE SHOULDERS OF THE NIGHT. THE MUSIC WIDENS ||

THE DOOR CLOSES SOFTLY, A SLOWLY WINKING EYE

ANGEL

An Invitation to Attend the Ball

SOUNDTRACK: *Son of a Preacher Man,* Dusty Springfield

THE RINSE ESTATE, EARLY EVENING. POV ANGEL LOOKING UP AT A DENOMINATION OF BOY-BOYS. BEHIND THEM LIGHTS SNIGGER & LIT WINDOWS CLOSE THEIR EYES. THE BOY-BOYS UNROLL AN INSULT LIKE A RED CARPET.

You belong in Maryville...

SOUND EFFECT: SLOW ECHO & REVERB *'you belong, belong, be_'*

GRADUAL CROSS FADE TO A BLOOD DROPLET LEAVING ANGEL'S LIP WITHOUT LOOKING BACK. THE CAMERA HUNCHES LOW & FOLLOWS THE TRAIL AS IT RACES ACROSS TOWN TOWARD THE MARYVILLE. CROSS CUT TO INTERIOR, NIGHTTIME. FULL FRAME CLOSE-UP OF INNER DOORS OF THE BAR. THERE IS A PAUSE THEN ANGEL BURSTS THROUGH THEM LIKE A NEWBORN. AS SHE ENTERS MUSIC OPENS ITS ECSTATIC ARMS.

EXTREME CLOSE-UP OF ANGEL'S SMILE, WHICH WIDENS UNTIL IT BECOMES THE NEXT SCENE.

MARYVILLE

A Word We Do Not Know

'a paradox of freedom and containment'

& we are all mouth existing in the breath between strangers muttered on the late night omnibus sewn into the fabric of embroidery club hidden in the architecture semaphore in the art works tongues like discreet slips of paper opened in corners backs turned *Maryville* we whisper & mean it & the air gathers air & becomes us a march of ghost women garishly invisible pulling off aprons slicking down hair leaving the houses that haunt us all across the blank city doors opening like arms drawn toward the idea of ourselves call it sex call it prayer we are a word we do not know we trip over ourselves in the dark we parenthesisters wondering if we were herded here if freedom is also a prison.

outside boy-boys call & call their song a choir of ring pulls kissing teeth.

MISE-EN-SCÈNE

Maryville 1957

|| BLACK & WHITE FILM. DOLLY SHOT: JACK BIRTHS THROUGH THE DOOR ||

INTERIOR, MARYVILLE. EVENING. JACK HESITATES ON THE THRESHOLD SCANNING THE ROOM.

THERE IS A SILENCE FILLED WITH DANCING.

A HOLY OF SNOWGLOBES ARE DISPLAYED BEHIND THE BAR ON HIGH SHELVING, AND THE BAR TOP IS CARPENTERED FROM LIBERATED CHURCH PEWS. A PARLIAMENT OF PUMPS HUDDLE TOGETHER IN THE CENTRE, WHISPERING ABOUT EACH NEW VISITOR. LOW TABLES PUNCTUATE THE BAR FLOOR IN FULL STOPS, EACH CROWDED WITH WOMEN UNAFRAID OF THEIR FACES.

THE LIGHT IS INDECENT, HARDLY DRESSED. SUITED BOIS STAND BAR SIDE PEERING INTO CRYSTAL BALLS OF BEER. AN OLD SILVERBACK SEARCHES FOR HER FACE IN THE RUBBLE OF THE EVENING. FEMMES WEAR DRESSES LIKE BULLFIGHTERS HOLD CAPES. INVERTS PESTER THEIR PROFILES & SCATTER SMILES LIKE ROLLS OF SHILLINGS TOWARD RUBY. SHE CATCHES ONE & POCKETS IT, HER WINK A CLAPPER BOARD. THE BAR/TENDER NODS AT RUBY WHO HANDS HER A WHISPER.

MARYVILLE LISTENS. AS ONE EACH WOMAN PLACES HER DRINK GENTLY ON THE TABLE & REVOLVES TO LOOK AT JACK. THE BAR TENDER THROWS A TEA TOWEL ACROSS THEIR HEADS TOWARD HER.

Hey. she says. *Jack.* she says

Catch.

THE CAMERA BECOMES THE TEA TOWEL AS IT LAUNCHES OVER THE HEADS OF THE REGULARS & INTO THE SUPRISED HANDS OF THE NEWLY NAMED JACK CATCH.

|| REVERSE CAMERA ANGLE POV JACK CATCH ||

AS SHE CATCHES IT, MARYVILLE BURSTS INTO BEING. THE BLACK & WHITE FILM EXPLODES INTO FULL TECHNICOLOUR, EACH OBJECT THE CAMERA MOVES PAST BECOMING RADIANT & EXACT, TRUE AS GIN, EVERYTHING IT TOUCHES COMING TO LIFE. THE CAMERA FLICKS THROUGH THE FIGURES AT THE BAR AS THOUGH GOING THROUGH ITS ADDRESS BOOK, FINALLY RESTING AT THE SILHOUETTE OF A WOMAN SHAPED LIKE A KEYHOLE. JACK WONDERS WHAT SHE UNLOCKS. SHE BALANCES AT THE END OF THE BAR SMOKING A LONG PINK CIGARETTE & BLOWING A SMOKE RING TOWARD JACK, WHICH HOOKS AROUND HER NECK. THE CAMERA TRAVELS SOHO'S LEGS TO HER FACE.

|| CHOKER SHOT OF SOHO'S OBSCURED FACE, FALLING INTO ITS UNENDING BLACK ||

CUT.

SOHO

Hi Femme

Soho wipes her lips on a plain boi
& casts them over her shoulder

to land in the seat beside the other
discarded unique hearted, she is

above all things The Cuntess
bodies buried all over her body

her high heels num-chuks
her eyes circled like wagons

blusher shade Khmer Rouge No5
not for the male gaze but the female gays

her fishnets trawl the dancefloor
picking up lost & blinking things

to sushi or breathe new life into
she once killed two stones with one bird

& tells Jack it is a rite of passage *her passage*
laughs like a rewound VCR as Jack neatly folds her face

Soho has sat on the same stool for decades
lit cigarette in her right extended hand

the Statue of Libertine, atemporal
around her, skin falls like empires

but she rains constant, a warm snow
whispering to the ghosts gathering in drifts

tapping a chrome red fingernail
against the chest of a snow globe.

DUDIZILE

Mr Ben

FADE UP ON DUDIZILE IN THE TAILOR'S SHOP. SHE IS
FULLY SUITED IN AN ENGLISH TWEED & IS EXAMINING
HER BRUTAL GLAMOUR IN THE FULL-LENGTH MIRROR.

Last night
she dreamed
she gave birth
to a suit
a pink flannel
slim shoulder
three-piece
that slid
into her hands
good weight
clear eyes
wet nose
that she raised
as her own
teaching it
the right way
to weigh thought
how to hold its shape
in public
to appear resolute
when she wakes
she is suffused
in a sweat

she could sew buttons
to & takes the dream
to the shop
where the air
has a perfect crease
& there is reason
the quantum physics
of couture
Dudz knows
the mirror thinks
about her
when she is not
there she is
examining its
impassive face
as if it is a developing
tray when Jack Catch
appears striding
forward out of it
arms held to her sides
captive soldier
brave face
Dudz takes her tape
& measures the distance
between one shoulder
& a family the collar bone
to Sunday School
the radius from tongue
to the grenade in her
chest she releases
Jack into the shape
of herself

Dudz thinks
that the whites
who litter the city
are lint
on a good jacket
but this one
is her negative
reverse reflection
they leave the shop
sewn together now
& walk toward
the violet
hello of Maryville

EPISODE TWO, SEASON ONE

1977 – 1987

rebels with a clause

MISE-EN-SCÈNE

1977-1987

SOUNDTRACK: *Mighty Real*, Sylvester

EXTERIOR, NIGHT. THE MARYVILLE BAR.

|| THE CAMERA ZOOMS IN ON THE PINK NEON SIGN THEN DRIFTS DOWN TO THE CLOSED DOORS. THE SALOON DOORS GESTATE. A NEW ERA IS BORN. CAMERA PUSHES THROUGH THE DOORS & DOLLIES THE BAR ||

inside / women have left their breasts at home / & brought someone else's teeth / femmes wear their hair / like a borough wears a riot / a quiver of butches / gaze at handprinted fanzines / their faces notice boards / that others leave their problems pinned to / a new band member / a meet up in the feminist library / Wild Court / a room in a co-op / a Brixton squat plotted / someone has a spare rib / & we grow from it / there is the scent of Greenham Common / an an*sistral* fire / burning somewhere stage left / a group of unfinished faces / hunch the floor / curled around placards / a chorus of thick pens choiring / headlines drip into t-shirts / & the music mutates / into a violence you can tap your feet to / make-up arrives / & swarms across the women / lips as cordoned off crime scenes / eyes fixed in the expression / of a slasher heroine's last hurrah / hair, a predator / jeans torn into chant / slogan mouth / while the mirror ball casts ghosts / across us.

|| CLOSE ANGLE OF JACK CATCH BEHIND THE BAR, POLISHING SNOWGLOBES. SHE OPENS AN EMPTY ONE & PLACES A CHARGE SHEET IN IT. SHE TAKES DOWN ANOTHER, AND POSITIONS A WHITE HANDKERCHIEF WITH A LIPSTICK KISS IN ITS CENTRE. THE LAST ONE, SHE FILLS WITH SMOKE FROM HER CIGARETTE, THE IDEA OF AFTERSHAVE ||

RUBY

The Door

|| CUT TO MEDIUM SHOT: RUBY STANDING ON THE THRESHOLD OF THE MARYVILLE, WEARING A PEA COAT & TRILBY SCANNING THE HORIZON ||

// Ruby guards the door like she guards her girl / pulls it closer to her / knowing the best way to call a man to you / is to not call him at all / (there is nothing as open / as a closed door) */ Ladies Night /* she growls / her tongue a visa / her chest a country / with its own border guards / Ruby is the space between words / no man's land / an intellectual concept / she flicks men off the door step / like flies from an antelope's eye / noting there is a ballet to men's violence / & she has dressed for the occasion / for the violet opera / knowing a fist begins at the grin / the boy-boys try to talk her into a girl / offer bouquets of cigarettes / punched lines / try to talk her out of her own mouth / & once / she listened // that night / the windows splintered into a thousand / dropped pint glasses / each one / refracting a rainbow / a stone rolling into the centre of the room //

MISE-EN-SCÈNE

Thank You Strange Lady

NIGHT, INTERIOR, MARYVILLE TOILETS.

|| POV: CAMERA OPENS CUBICLE DOOR. CLOSE-UP OF A YOUNG WOMAN, VOMITING IN A TOILET BOWL. A HAND HOLDS HER HAIR BACK ||

it is a quarter to you / & in the toilets / an ancient ritual repeats / a hand holds a beehive back from a face / the girl's make-up has run / found a better place to live / she yells to a god / she hopes doesn't exist / as an avalanche races down white slopes of porcelain / there / the elder femme says / there / let it out girl / & her hair begins to scroll / now a pixie cut / now a stage curtain dropping / now a suburban Mohican / a skin head & quiff / a demi wave, & on / the same hand / browsing the years / girls vomiting girls / full grown & stubborn / onto the bright lap of Maryville

LIGHTS FLICKER LIKE SHOW TUNES. SLOW FADE & REPEAT.

SOHO

a flock of femmes alight a field

INTERIOR, MARYVILLE, LATE EVENING.

|| WIDE SHOT OF THE LONG PEW OF THE BAR. THE BOIS HAVE BEEN EVICTED FROM THEIR BAR STOOLS BY A FLOCK OF WILD FEMMES, WHO TOSS THE CAMERA BETWEEN THEM LIKE HAWK BAIT ||

The Femmedem gather in squarrel
Lambrini as a mixer, She Guevaras

beneath the cataract mirror ball
wrangling disco bladder & unkempt tongue

an acrylic tipped with snow
their hair, a personal bodyguard

a topiary of the Risen Christ
their mouths, red ships leaving

fixing their make-up even though it's not broken
& bois, young & unfinished, swarm & shiver

throw punches in the air & juggle them
bursting the banks of their belonging

bigger now, cocky as cocaine cockatoos
they let their lips unravel into catwalks

& the Femmedem stalk up them;
one boi brave as bank holidays

turns to Soho & says, she says, the boi says
take a night off your face love

& Soho looks up, makes the air sit down
pins the bois to their bodies

peeling them until they are exposed:
girls in suits in a vast ballroom at the end of the world

Soho stands, more objection than object
straightens her hem, throttles her coat

says: *I'm leaving darling.*
the light is too heterosexual this evening

& smiles to Jack, her lips two lines across a mirror.

THE BOIS

Penetration is Oppression

the old bois watch
faces sump water
as a procession of protesters
bewilder the bar, steering
between the island
tables, detouring through
legs, across the bar top
slaloming the pumps
around the toilet pedestals
& back through the heart
of Maryville, placards
of their own faces
a living obituary
fields of violets pouring from
their mouths
littering the floor
with women's centres & refuges
community meetings &
queer bookshops,
Ruby thinks that
from above they are a sailor's
figure-eight, half hitch
Jack nods:
everyone is a thought experiment
she whispers
wearing their deaths on their chest
a black t-shirt with a pink triangle

scuffed leather jeans
cuffs turned up like waves
a surf of white sock
9-hole doctor martins
laces dark as mid-morning
Tuesday, brandishing their gay
ears & dancing the lambda
& on they weave
now a conga line of clippers
shaving their own
heads, & the old bois glamour
pick tobacco from their nails
worry the air, hide
in each other's eyebrows
confused by the
applause of closet doors
the riot at the heart of each
how visible they are
how flick knife their smiles
are whether the
umbrella will bring
the rain.
Jack just fancies women
this one in particular
she smiles encouragingly at Soho
who takes her smile
& fashions it into a handbag.
But now here comes the night
carrying morning in its mouth
& the conga line picks up
pace, threads the protesters
to the bar, sewing

the personal to the political
more women join
the infinite line
that loops the bar
in lemniscate
before straightening
out again, a line
of enraged & enamoured
feral & exact
who march & march
& march, straight into
the fin-de-siecle
of Angel's nostrils.

        THE SALOON DOORS CHATTER ALL NIGHT.

JACK CATCH

2 x 10

Tonight / the bar is a pop-up book / & Jack sighs / polishing snow globes / washing tongues / as women mythologise themselves / they look at her in a red love / damned by disapproval / there are mutters abroad / of how their suits / are not armour but bruising / how their faces / belong to their fathers / how they are not women / but women who are not men / which is different / & throughout it all / through the demonstrations / through contraception & cervical hijack / through mountains of bras burning / through nuclear missiles & obscenity laws / Jack's hair is stoic / picketing her head / shaved each eve / with the edges of smashed / nights / white hairs beginning their ascent / across the bois / as though slowly being rubbed out / fault lines trouble their faces / they catch each other's eyes / & raise them as their own / shrug / these young things / glamouring / voices like lift music / Jack throws back her head / & the old bois howl / alongside the boy-boys outside / who stop for a moment / quizzing the wind / then resume their night alphabet / throwing air in to the air.

ANGEL

Shadow Boxing

warm pisslight of the all night café / Angel fights her shadow / & the shadow wins / but still she dances a drill / face to the wall / muscles like twisted tea towels / shuffle & pendulum / her shadow is leaving her / has left a note by the bread bin / bob & weave / fists rising like a natural disaster / Angel / stands in awe of her ascendance / pivot / feet together zig zag / she throws a punch into orbit / & it is drawn into the black hole of the shadow / alongside tongues torn from their moorings / the back seats of school buses / her girl / the punch parades / the lacuna dressed as her father / shouting orders / urging her on / see how she is almost / almost / see how she puts her shoulder into her hand / casts it into a hook / & releases / the café door chimes / behind her / her shadow / slumped to the lino.

THE BOIS

Cock Sonnets

SLOW FADE TO INTERIOR MARYVILLE, MID MORNING. THE BOIS ARE GATHERED AROUND A SMALL BROWN PAPER PACKAGE DISPLAYED ON A LOW CABARET TABLE. SOHO WATCHES LIKE A TOURIST INSTAGRAMMING APOCALYPSE.

(i) a strange visitor

before the bar opens that day
the old bois discover
a strange visitor & hunker
the dildo as if it were a kitten
what will it eat? where will it sleep?
what if it tries to find its way home?
Soho watches through slot machine eyes
as the bois give commands it ignores
tag it, teach it to beg, to make the bed
she knows things get lost in the triangle
all night banging the wet drum
this square peg. this bridge
if Jack held her eye to the hole
she might find herself looking back.

(ii) the naming ceremony

Jack & Soho's first ebullient child
is a dildo stiff, black as tongues
the squat general, Mr Commissar
first man in, last man to leave
Soho balances it on the draining board
& Jack oils it carefully in the lager light
how can loving a thing also destroy it?
this their glorious heir righteous
there is a raffle for names in the bar
a moving ceremony at the lock in
but beneath her suit Jack's skin
rears like horses in books girls
read, what would it be like to be
touched, to be reimagined, real.

(iii) the good uncles

Dudizile & Valentine
are godparents & babysit the cock
a shoulder draped in a white tea-towel
they pat its sticky back, check for colic
pass it to each other like a well-fed spliff
take it for walks in the boarded-up park
to play with the invisible trees
a strange blooming at the centre of each
like sunrise at the after party
as it kicks its legs on the swing
screaming higher, higher
later they each feel a violent loss

what is the word for grieving something
that is still alive, a present absence?

(iv) the sex wars

Jack dotes on her child
Soho less so, is elegantly bored
by the constant squall & need
by the way it slips its harness
& races through the streets
shrieking for a mate, leaving
Soho listless, waiting at the window
beyond the roof tops the sex
war rages, feminists in balaclavas
bludgeon sado-masochists in balaclavas
it's all rhetorical, even the blood.
Soho stretches, don't they know
it is the same war that always rages
across the body of woman.

SOHO

the flight of the femmes

INTERIOR, MARYVILLE, IN THE FULL THROAT OF A SATURDAY NIGHT WELL LIVED. CIRCLES OF LIGHT CAST BY THE MIRROR BALL RICOCHET THE ROOM LIKE BULLETS, LEAVING SMALL HOLES IN THE CENTRE OF THE BOIS.

in the hour before closing
        the room ignites

                into a flock of wild femmes
                      lipstick flamingos

                red mouths in murmuration
                      making the shapes of wings

a flutter of soft labia
        the scent of lost mothers

                see the girls: wading in high heels
                      calf deep in the still waters

                of the dancefloor, fishing
                      for a scattering of eyes

that eclectic dart of recognition
        tongue like a shoal of minnows

        there are things at the bottom
                of the dance floor that do not see well

        that know our names but cannot say them
                old bois, the bent resistance

the flight of femmes soar above us
        to perch on the lighting rig

        dropping lavender sprigs from pink beaks
                that nestle into the soil of the dancefloor

        twitch & shoot upward into slipknots
                of unravelling femmes

who hurtle to the creased ceiling
        spilling cracked jokes

        winks become cartoon birds laying eggs
                that hatch, acrylic first, into more femmes

        & suddenly / o god / they are flocking / yes
                blood birds brazen & rising

arching like eyebrows
        over thin-lipped roof tops

                heading inexorably
                        into the cervix of the sun

JACK CATCH

Moon over Charing Cross Road

There are starlings in the blood today / Jack can feel their dissolve / the pull toward new shapes / a sullen Rorschach under skin / now a moth / now a child torn between the mouths of parents / now a silver moon illuminating a pensive butch / heading to the bar / with a towerblock of books / tracing the walk of letters: *Compulsory Heterosexuality and Lesbian Existence* / opening the cover and falling in / there are dark tunnels in the book / that lead back to herself / & Jack walks them slowly / led by her lit zippo / no matter how many routes she takes / there is no way out of the book / not now / it is 1982 / & a vague riot is coughing within / small fires dot her roadside / leading to a cluster of camps / gathered together like charms on a razor wire bracelet / wrapped around the wrist of a cruise missile / it is true, she thinks / Greenham women are everywhere / letting go of the hands of children / to take hold of the hands of children / abandoning life / in order to find it / & missiles are everywhere too / in the camp / at the bus stop / in the classroom / peering between net curtains / beside you in bed / Jack understands why books have covers / it is to stop them / one learned thing / leads to another / & Jack's head is a red balloon on the end of a string / it floats above the counter / all day / considering the shapes beneath / how they fit together / how they don't / while across the bar / women gather around campfires tables / warming their doctorates.

|| VALENTINE EXITS THE BAR IN TO THE BROAD HELLO OF ALIVE, & THE CAMERA FOLLOWS HER IN ONE CONTINUOUS SHOT ||

MISE-EN-SCÈNE

Valentine Finds Railton Road

SOUNDTRACK: *The Guns of Brixton,* The Clash

INTERIOR, TUBE STATION. A TUBE EASES INTO A PLATFORM LIKE 70s SOFT PORN.

|| COWBOY SHOT: TUBE DOORS OPEN AND VALENTINE STEPS TO THE PLATFORM. HER HAIR HAS GROWN INTO AN AFRO THE SHAPE OF A GREAT BLACK CAT. SHE CARRIES IT WITH HER ALWAYS. LEAVES SLITHERS OF MEAT FOR IT ON HER SHOULDER. VALENTINE'S HAIR CONJURES ROAR & RESISTANCE, A DISSIDENT SHADOW ||

|| FOCUS PULL: VALENTINE ON THE ESCALATOR. FROM THIS ANGLE IT LOOKS AS THOUGH THE ESCALATOR LEADS TO A HEAVEN, OR A HOLE IN THE CELL WALL ||

CAMERA TRACKS OUT OF BRIXTON TUBE STATION, TURNING LEFT. AN EVANGELIST RELEASES A RUPTURED SYMPHONY AT THE LENS, BUT WE PUSH PAST. THERE IS A DANCE TO THE AIR, A KINDLY FURY. THE COLOUR IS UPRISING. THE SOUND IS KALEIDOSCOPIC, THE AIR STURDY ENOUGH TO FALL INTO THE ARMS OF.

|| POV VALENTINE: FOCUS ON STREET SIGN *'COLDHARBOUR LANE'* ||

SHE TURNS DOWN COLDHARBOUR LANE INTO A THICKNESS OF BODY & LIGHT; REGGAE MUSIC WANDERS THE HOT STREET AS THOUGH LOOKING FOR SOME SHADE. EVERY FACE THAT VALENTINE PASSES HAS A FACE THAT KNOWS WITHOUT KNOWING, THAT IS THE SAME AND OTHER IN THAT EXACT MOMENT. VOICES POUR ON TO THE PAVEMENT FROM INSIDE THE PRINCE ALBERT PUB AND COLLECT IN A POOL AT HER FEET. SHE STEPS OVER THEM AND WALKS TOWARD THE BRIDGE. SHE CROSSES THE ROAD.

|| POV VALENTINE: FOCUS ON STREET SIGN *'RAILTON ROAD'* ||

WE WALK ALONG A ROW OF TERRACED HOUSES, SOME WITH SHOP FRONTS BUT MOST IN A STATE OF ABANDON AND DISMISSAL. THEY ARE THE LAST PEOPLE STANDING AT AN ALL-NIGHT RAVE. SOME OF THE WINDOWS ARE COVERED BY BLANKETS AS THOUGH SOMEONE INSIDE WORRIES ABOUT THEM AT NIGHT.

OUR PACE QUICKENS UNTIL WE STAND IN FRONT OF NUMBER 121. VALENTINE LOOKS UP AT THE HOUSE. ITS DOWNSTAIRS IS AN OLD SHOP FRONT MESHED. FLYERS AND POSTERS TATTOO THE BUILDING. THE FRONT DOOR HAS A BOOT PRINT BY THE HANDLE AND A HOLE LEFT BY A POLICE BATON. THE DOOR SMILES IN RECOGNITION & VALENTINE STEPS IN.

VALENTINE

On Railton Road

i

& sometimes when you enter a room you are walking into yourself & the walls know your name & the carpet understands your feet & the skirting board doesn't get embarrassed if you speak out of turn & the furniture recognises your body & the kettle sings in a language few speak & the other people in the room are also people who live inside your body but you never knew never knew.

ii

Valentine sits cross legged / in a circle of other Others / rolling spliffs / from the pages of the Female Eunuch / the Scum Manifesto / & chopping up lines / of debate / slowly untangling her body / from her theory / analysis can get stuck between the teeth / but she is unlearning so very much / unravelling like a jumper caught on barbed wire / saturnine on the dead body of the sofa / cup of pursed-lip tea & soya milk / at her feet / revolution should have better toilets / she thinks / but says nothing / just smokes / holding an eye to each ring / as though monocle / as though seeing clearly for the first time.

iii

while the feminists deconstruct / Valentine tames her hands / teaches them new tricks / already they can smell / approval on the horizon / noses quivering / as she imagines what they might construct / out of cast-off theory & old harrows of argument / whether she can rewire the squat / using only invective / if polemic will clear the pipes this time / she enrols in a carpentry course / & becomes / liberating shelves & simple tables from the wood / finding a home / in the way things join.

iv

the table is a perfect / o / a circle / so that no one is the leader / so that both mouths speak / are valued / & Valentine imagines the table / as a cervix / a birthing point / & wonders what they will call themselves now / if they are black / or women / if they are lesbian / or underclass / which part of themselves / they will fight for first / someone speaks of segregation / & another of disorder / the animal courts / men with tongues like lit fuses / warnings of approaching storms of white locust / & Valentine wonders / at the awe of this new engine / they dismantle the day / until it lays in parts before them on the table / Valentines zips her leather into a pout / & leaves / the space on the table / filled as soon as she stands / women are water, she thinks / but even water needs something to hold it.

ANGEL

Rapture

CUT TO CRAMPED INTERIOR OF A TOILET CUBICLE IN THE MARYVILLE. ANGEL SITS ON THE CLOSED LID HOLDING THE DOOR SHUT WITH ONE BOOT. IT BANGS BUT SHE IGNORES IT. SHE IS RACKING UP A LINE OF COCAINE ON A THIGH OF HER LEATHER TROUSERS.

Maryville is a holy space
pink sacrament

& Angel a Crystal Methodist worshipping
at the altar of austere excess

the body become powder
become liquid & thrill

wine become water become dance
exogenic & ecstatic, ritual & chance

leaving her body
to find her body

among the suburban subalterns
amphetamine queens cocaine kings

track marks along her inner arm
like starling prints across snow

not raving   but drowning
tonight   Angel will cut her past into lines

etch them into a family tree on the toilet seat
tonight   Angel will take a woman

like a screenshot   like a pill tonight
Angel will rise   far above herself

the resurrection of the numb
the rapture o lord the rapture.

CAMERA TILTS SLOWLY UPWARD TOWARD A FIZZING FLOURESCENT LIGHT. SOMETHING IS TRAPPED IN THERE. FROM THIS DISTANCE & IN THIS LIGHT, IT LOOKS LIKE ANGEL.

MISE-EN-SCÈNE

London Fields: The Lesbians Are Coming[ix]

SOUND: SOMETHING PATHE, SOMETHING TYPE-WRITER. AN INTRUSION OF TRUMPET.

LIBRARY FOOTAGE OF THE GREAT BRITISH PICNIC. PLATOONS OF FAMILIES EAT OFF UNION JACKS CAST OVER THE GRASS OF LONDON FIELDS. THE CAMERA SWOOPS OVER THEM LIKE A BLUEBIRD.

VOICE OVER, ACCENT RECEIVED PRONUNCIATION CIRCA 1950S:

They are a happy bunch! They sing all day and dance all night!

CAMERA ZOOMS IN ON ONE FAMILY. THEIR SMILES ARE QUICHE. THEIR CHILDREN ARE STATIC, FIXED IN A MOMENT OF BLAND JOY. THERE ARE CUPCAKES DECORATED WITH PAGE 3 MODELS.

VOICE OVER:

The British are the only animals who eat themselves. Found living in the cracks in conversation, they queue to stalk themselves for years before launching their attack. But now something new is coming to London.

CAMERA ZOOMS OUT TO TAKE IN A BACKGROUND OF DERELICT HOUSES, OLD BOMB CRATERS, WILD

GRASSES FLOWERING IN SHOP WINDOWS.

ZOOM IN ON A CRACK IN A SHOP WINDOW. IT IS FRACTURED INTO THE SHAPE OF THE LONDON UNDERGROUND. AS WE WATCH, THE CRACK ANIMATES & TINY TUBE TRAINS ARE SHOWN MIGRATING FROM THE CENTRE OF LONDON TO THE EDGES OF THE CITY, PERISTALTIC THROUGH THE INTESTINAL UNDERGROUND.

VOICE OVER:

It is 1979 & the capital's population is at its lowest point since the war. Unemployment, inflation, and bad investment pierces a hole in the economy through which ordinary people fall. But something strange is coming, some odd revolution. All over the country women are packing their belongings into their mouths and heading toward the deserted houses. They break the locks in the dead of chatter & move themselves & their ravenous ideas in. Soon London Fields, Broadway Market & Dalston are squatted by hundreds of badly dressed women, bolt cutting their hair, sharing childcare like spliffs, & rewiring their faulty politics. Over 50 lesbian squats spread across the area, terraced houses linking arms like women at peace camps, like chromosomes.

WOMEN IN BLUNT CLOTHING ARE SHOWN SITTING AT TABLES SHARING SOYA MILK TEA, SAT CROSSED LEGGED ETCHING PLACARDS WITH PLACEBOS, PASSING SPANNERS BETWEEN THEM LIKE SPECULUM, DIVIDING & REUNITING, DILATING, MULTIPLYING, VIRAL.

the Bent Resistance Attends a Stop the Clause[x] Meeting

at the lesbian & gay centre[xi] / leaflets are passed around like vol-au-vents / as a man argues with his own face / & loses / while another accuses their clothing of sedition / they eye Soho in her red dress of dissent / Jack in her 3-piece suit / sewn from the skin of colonial England / (she is the best room in the house) / Valentine's bewildered leathers / tight as a goosestep / they are too sexual / it seems / for a discussion about sexuality / Soho flashes her clause / & Jack winks / they are an odd inheritance / these an-sissys / handed down like necklaces / to a generation who will never wear them / these inalienable gays / who will grow up to / abseil down the sheer precipice of common politics / who will chain themselves to the news / who will form an orderly queue in Manchester / that has still not reached its head / who have given blood / & now will give blood / who will win everything by losing / but this night / the dark is full of more dark / & they leave quietly / like women / wondering if they have the right / to want rights / scuff faced & ill tongued as they are / they wander London's closeted streets / French kissing the open mouths of bottles / until they find themselves / staring up at Portcullis House / where all the little men cog / milling their small lies / pointing at one another / cottaging at the weekend / Soho leans against its wall / a streetlamp star system / ingenue on a giro / rebel with a clause / & paints her lips / like a murderer / like a line around a body / Jack startles / but Soho keeps going / straight off her face / & onto the wall / in writing as red as hands:

fight for the right to make life poetry[xii]

indeed / the bois think / indeed / Jack removes her jacket / & drapes it over / Soho's shoulders / it is the tiny activisms / the quiet revolutions / that make the war bearable.

LONG SHOT OF JACK, SOHO, DUDZ & ANGEL AS THEY HEAD INTO THE QUIET DARK. FROM THIS ANGLE THEY LOOK LIKE SCRATCHES AGAINST A CELL WALL.

SOHO

Another Nail on the Cross at Calvary

|| WIDE ANGLE OF INTERIOR MARYVILLE. A SOFT NIGHT. THE MUSIC HAS LOOSENED ITS TIE & IS LOUNGING ON A BANQUETTE, A SMALL TUMBLER OF WHISKY BEFORE IT. THE BAR IS SLOW THIS EVENING. SOHO PERCHES ON HER PEDESTAL AT THE END OF THE BAR, WHILE JACK POLISHES THE FINGERPRINTS FROM HER FINGERS. THE CAMERA FOCUSSES ON SOHO FROM A SEAT BESIDE THE MUSIC ||

light deflects
from Soho's
apex acrylics
colliding
with the eyes
of each boi
in the bar who
shake their
squint & duck
as though
they can
throw away
light but she
has them
now, maybe
start a fire
her nails
sculptural

sepulchral
Swiss army knives
each acrylic
set with
a small silver
tool a tiny
saw an awl
a corkscrew
a fish scaler
a handbag
a gun
the key
to your
house
you
it is said
that she
matches
her friends
to her nails
& we believe it
she perches
at the end
of the bar
wearing her
pocket butch
lighting her
cigarette
from the flames
inside quiet
bois blowing
clouds across

the bar
that drizzle
slow songs.

LIBRARY FOOTAGE

SUDDEN CUT TO A MONTAGE OF MICROFICHE NEWS-PAPER FRONT PAGES SHRILLING THEIR RED. THE HEADLINES SPRINT ACROSS THE SCREEN, EACH ONE BULLYING THE OTHER FROM VIEW TO TAKE IS PLACE.

-andinothernews*islesbiansexillegal*Therightsexofthepatient wasunknownuntilSaturdaywhenthe patientwasfoundtobea womanHerhairwascroppedlikeamannooneknewmeasanything otherthanasamanAwomaninMaleAttireAtWandsworthPOLICE CourtonSaturdayLucyShawmarriedwhow asdressedinmale attirewaschargedwithbeingdrunkanddisorderlyMrBridgere markedthatitwasan actofgreatindecencybesidesbeingapublic offenceWearetalkingaboutsexpracticesand**lesbian**bestiality WearetalkingaboutafloodofpermissivePORNOGRAPHYSelf confessed**lesbian**MPMaure enColquhounsaidanattemptisto madeintheCommonstoexpelfromtheBritishMedicalAssociation doctorswhoarrangedTESTTUBEbabiesfor**lesbian**couples*islesbian sexillegal*ThisisamoralmatterforsocietyasawholeNoto**lesbian** mumsHavealsotreatedwithsympathysubjectswhichwerepreviously tabooinTheKillingofSisterGeorgewhichportrays**lesbianism**asa partofliferatherthanaviceThe atrecensorshipwasparticularly strictonhomosexualityandthedepictionofgaymenandwomen onst agePOLICEbelieve**lesbian**extremistsmayhaverapeda33 yearoldmanatknifepointVincentedelaF uentewassnatchedby twowomenashewalkedalongaMadridstreetASELFCONFESSED **lesbian**wasgrantedinterimcustodyatAberdeenSheriffCourt yesterdayofher14yearoldsonbutshewaswarnedthattheboyshould bebroughtupheterosexually*Islesbiansexillegal*inquiryintohow four**lesbian**protestersbreachedsecuritytotrytoDISRUPTalive newsbroadcastnewsreadersSueLawleyandNicholasWitchell

werepraisedfortheircoolhandlingofthestudioINVASIONWhat
is*lesbianism*?Whatcausesit?Canitbecured?Two**lesbians**have
beensackedbyanurseryschoolaftercomplaints*Islesbiansexillegal*
aboutdiscriminationagainstboysthereFacedastringofallegations
fromparentsTeacher**LESBIANS**areforcedtolivealiewithfamily
andfriendsGAMESTEACHERJayneScotttoldanOld Baileyjury
yesterdayMostDISTURBINGwasnottheswearingdrunksandthe
strongodourofcheapwinesbuttheflirting**lesbians**Homosexuals
and**lesbians**shouldnotbeallowedtoteachPolicemanquestionedin
lesbiandeathprobeAPOLICEconstablewaslastnightstillbeing
questionedbydetectives investigatingthedeathof**lesbian**vicegirl
ATTACKon**lesbian**lefthorrifyinginjuriesTheferociousclawhammer
attackon**lesbian**SusanCrakerhasleftherdependentonothersfor
therestofherlifeConsentingsexualrelationshipswithtwoothergirls
bothaged17andtoPROTECTthemfromtroublewiththeirfamilies
shedressedasaBOYAn18yearoldwomanisservingasixyearprison
senteneandinothern-

THE SPEED INCREASES AS THE FOOTAGE MOVES
FORWARD UNTIL THE FONT THICKENS INTO A BODY
OF POLICE SPRINTING INTO THE HANGING JAW OF
MARYVILLE, WHO REAPPLIES LIPSTICK AS THEY ENTER.

MISE-EN-SCÈNE

It says it's a girl

SOUNDTRACK: *The sound a bottle makes as it glides through the air.*

|| EXTREME WIDE SHOT, MARYVILLE LATE EVENING. ||

THE MUSIC IS FROZEN ON ONE LEG, STARING AT THE DOOR WHICH APPLAUDS A BATTALION OF POLICE. THEY PENETRATE THE BAR & THE WOMEN WITHIN STOP.

CUT TO CAMERA PAN OF BACK WALL, MARYVILLE.

butches are lined up / their hands / small birds migrating their bodies / three policemen pillory the line / shaking the bois like sauce bottles / searching for the woman / hiding in them / finding the female beneath bra straps / between the legs / the butches are Guernica / a still-living still-life / more story than body / this is the part we don't talk about / how his breath interrogates air / how a man whittles a woman / the laying on of hands / how the bois will not look at each other / the only remaining dignity / when they cry it is with their teeth / Cher Noble calls from the stage / *It looks like we have help with the washing up, girls*[xiii] / as a forest of black rubber gloves / blossom across the bar / sifting for meaning / their estranged mothers / they hold up a new born book / like a sacrifice / & squirrel its pages / a gram of thought / in a zip lock bag / & now the women / transform beneath their search / a face torn in two / a girl running through a red dust street / a young boi ancient with love / locked in the back of a wagon / a butch beaten by her shadow / while teachers hide in the toilets / alongside solicitors & sex workers / & femmes bat their eyelashes like the Ashes / Jack frisks her thoughts / sets down the globe she is polishing / says, *Gentlemen* / her eyes a closed tube station / too many things crammed in the closet / she thinks / we will never find what we are looking for / throughout history / always this / a door opens suddenly / & the whole world falls out.

|| CAMERA IS ANANMORPHIC, TAKING IN THE BAR ROOM, THE BUILDING, THE STREET, THE CITY, THE COUNTRY, THE WORLD THE WORLD THE WORLD ||

VALENTINE

Brixton Riots[xiv]

|| A WORLD CRADLED IN A CAMERA LENS, A PUPIL IN GOD'S EYE. WITHOUT WARNING THE CAMERA SHOT REVERSES AS THOUGH WE HAVE REACHED TENSION HORIZON IN AN ELASTIC BAND, & WE ARE CATAPULTED AT INCREASING SPEED BACK TOWARD THE WORLD, & INTO THE CENTRE OF COLDHARBOUR LANE IN BRIXTON, LONDON. TONGUES OF FIRE GOSSIP ABOUT THE POLICE, WHO STAND IN CLUTTER, CROUCHED BEHIND PERPSEX SHIELDS. WINDOWS ARE SMASHED INTO THE SHAPE OF THE UNION JACK. BATONS METRONOME, THE HEARTBEAT OF BRIXTON. ||

in this scene
Valentine skids

out of the flames
into the eye of the camera

the past riding pillion
its skinny arms around her waist

a simmering can of red stripe
hissing on the handlebars

& she is exact, a straight line
carrying anarchy in her mouth

around her the street spasms
& shop windows boil

young men ask to be young men
but they are skin instead

the police sweep them up
like pennies from a side table

there are big words for how she feels tonight
but she has dropped them somewhere

instead, she rides, aviators two pools of burn
as she considers how leathers retain shape

holding body when she cannot
how skin remembers, thinks.

when she steps out of them
they stand in the hallway all night

mewling for her return, sentinel
& maybe she cooks them breakfast

before clicking herself back into them
& heading back into the sad joy

to gather with a liability of lesbians
beneath an anal moon

the worst riots are the silent ones
Valentine says

like the one next to you now
just there darling. just there.

THE FLAMES FROM BURNING CARS SLOWLY CROSS FADE INTO TWINKLING FAIRY LIGHTS ON AN ARTIFICIAL CHRISTMAS TREE.

MISE-EN-SCÈNE

A Maryville Christmas

SOUNDTRACK: *The Fairy Tale of New York,* The Pogues

INTERIOR MARYVILLE. MORNING.

|| DOLLY SHOT ALONG A LONG TABLE, PEOPLED BY BUTCHES & FEMMES, THE INDETERMINATE, PLUS JACK CATCH, VALENTINE, ANGEL, SOHO, DUDZILE, RUBY, & VALENTINE'S TWO BROTHERS. CHRISTMAS MUSIC IS PLAYING. THE SCENE CROSS FADES TO:

WIDE ANGLE. BACK BAR OF THE MARYVILLE ||

THEY DECORATE THE FAMILY TREE, HANGING TAMPONS SPRAYED IN ANTIQUE GOLD FROM EACH BRANCH, & IMPALING AN EAGLE EYE ACTION MAN ON TOP. DUDZ HAS CUT HIM A TINY LEATHER HARNESS. SOHO SETS A CANDELABRA WITH RED CANDLES ON THE TABLE & LIGHTS HER CIGARETTE OFF IT. A PACKAGE HOLIDAY OF GRINNING FAIRY LIGHTS WAVE THEIR ARMS ACROSS THE BAR. A RAINBOW BEGINS ITS ARC TOWARD THE TABLE, THEN THINKS BETTER OF ITSELF. MUSIC NURSES A PINT, ROCKS & REPEATS ITSELF. JACK CATCH & VALENTINE CARRY FOOD TO THE TABLE. THIS IS THE FEAST OF ST GIRO, THE MARYVILLE TRADITIONAL BUFFET FOR SEASONAL STRAYS. IT IS PAID FOR BY THE REGULARS: A PEWTER PINT MUG HANDED AROUND, MONTH AFTER MONTH, & STUFFED

WITH SHRAPNEL THAT TRANSITIONS SLOWLY INTO FINGER ROLLS & TINNED SALMON, POTTED MEATS AND CELERY STICKS, SUGARED LETTUCE, & HOMEMADE PRAWN COCKTAIL. THE CENTRE PIECE IS A BIRD STUFFED WITH GOSSIP. THE TURKEY HAS A CLEAVAGE AND A MURDEROUS LOOK IN HER EYE. JACK BEGINS TO CARVE IT WITH THE THIN EDGE OF HER SMILE. DUDZ CAREFULLY DRESSES THE NAPKINS, CUT TO THE BIAS. VALENTINE POLISHES THE PLASTIC CUTLERY. ANGEL LAYS OUT THE COLLECTOR'S EDITION SILVER JUBILEE PLATES. THEIR FACES ARE UNOPENED PRESENTS. AFTERSHAVE MARRIES THE AIR. SOHO'S HAIR IS THE TREE.

|| CAMERA CHOKER SHOT OF EACH OF THE DINERS ||

THEY SIT DOWN TOGETHER & EAT THEIR FACES, THEIR TROUBLES, THE OVERDUE RENT, THE IMPOSSIBILITY OF LIVING, THE QUALITY OF AIR, HOW THE NIGHT IS NO LONGER QUITE SO NIGHT; THEY SIT TOGETHER & EAT THE YOUNG, THEIR UNENDING DEMONSTRATIONS, THE OBSCENITY ACT, SECTION 28, THEY BRING BOOKS TO THE TABLE ON A LARGE CATERING TROLLEY & DOUSE THEM IN BRANDY. WHEN THEY PULL THE CRACKER THERE IS A TINY PLASTIC SNOW GLOBE INSIDE.

|| CLOSE-UP ANGEL OPENING PUB DOOR ||

MEANWHILE ANGEL IS DREAMING OF A WHITE CHRISTMAS. SHE MEETS A MAN BETWEEN THE STARTERS AND THE MAIN.

|| CLOSE-UP OF CLOSED MARYVILLE PUB DOOR. A CHORUS OF BOY-BOYS SEMI CIRCLE IT ||

OUTSIDE SNOW FALLS IN LOVE WITH THE STREET. BOY-BOYS HOWL THEIR INFINITE CAROLS.

MISE-EN-SCÈNE

Angel

SOUNDTRACK: *I am Dreaming of a White Christmas,* Bing Crosbie

EXTERIOR NIGHT, OUTSIDE MARYVILLE BAR. THE DOOR HAS BEEN LEFT ON ITS LATCH. LIGHT WRIGGLES FREE & ILLUMINATES THE FACES OF FOUR MEN, GATHERING AROUND EACH OTHER'S BREATH FOR WARMTH. CUT TO POV ANGEL WALKING BACK TOWARD MARYVILLE, A TINY WHITE CHRISTMAS CARD IN HER HAND. SHE SEES THE CHOIR OF BOY-BOYS WHO SING THEIR INANITIES TO DEAD GODS. CLOSE-UP ON ANGEL'S OPEN FACE.

my darling, petit cocaine king
                rumour has it

Angel once snorted the line
                for the toilet

strange how one line
                merges into another

lines in an exercise book
                lines in detention

line for the dole office
                punch lines in the bar

chat up lines before closing
                all those pretty white lines

becoming the lines
                in the middle of a road

that lead to a line drawn
                here on the ground

white lines around a body
                a line cordoning the public.

|| WIDE ANGLE BOY-BOYS. THEY TAKE OFF THEIR SMILES WHEN ANGEL PASSES & ONE LEANS FORWARD TO WHISPER. WE CANNOT HEAR WHAT HE SAYS. CAMERA SHOT CLOSE-UP ON ANGEL LOOKING BACK AT THEM, HAND ON THE DOOR. YELLOW LIGHT SINGS TO GREY SNOW ||

ANGEL

The Death of God

when the boy boys detain her / *excuse me love* / she is thinking of summer / how it feels when the air wants you / it has been snowing / *excuse me love* / & Angel notices one flake / drift slowly to the ground / its web / a frozen boxing ring / & it is all so beautiful / so luminous & alive / *excuse me love* / she smiles / & her smile is a door / & in they come / without wiping their feet / leaving their hats on their heads / in they come / a queue in her hallway / she cannot find room for them all / they are spilling off the living room furniture / they are becoming the carpet / & in they come / bursting the walls / making her hatless / & she cannot fit in her home anymore / they are pushing her out / each kick an eviction notice / in they come / push / push push into the dark unknowing / the blank everything / the bitter & sharp / the lightthelightthe lightwe-

FAMILY

Spilt / Screen

SOUNDTRACK: *Smalltown Boy*, Bronski Beat

SPLIT SCREEN BETWEEN OUTSIDE AND INSIDE THE MARYVILLE BAR, CHRISTMAS NIGHT 1987.

LEFT SCREEN:

TRACKING SHOT BETWEEN EACH CHARACTER OUTSIDE. CHOKER SHOT ON ANGEL. A FIGHT EXPLODES LIKE A BLIZZARD & THEY DANCE & DANCE. THE SNOW SITS DOWN & WATCHES AS THOUGH THROUGH A GAUZE CURTAIN. IT IS A BALLET, EACH OF THEIR BODIES FOLLOWING THE TRAJECTORY OF A SNOWFLAKE, PIRHOUETTING & DIZZYING TO THE COLD GROUND. THE SNOW DOES NOT GET UP AGAIN.

RIGHT SCREEN:

INSIDE THE MARYVILLE JACK IS SERVING HERSELF A PINT WHILE RUBY COMBS HER HAIR. VALENTINE'S BROTHERS PULL CRACKERS & DUDIZILE ORIGAMIS A SET OF PAPER CROWNS FOR THEM TO WEAR LATER. VALENTINE LOOKS DEEP INTO A GIRL'S EYES FORGETTING THEY HAVE ALREADY MET. SOHO IS SHARPENING HER FINGERNAILS WHEN SHE SUDDENLY STOPS & LOOKS UP, HER EYES FRESHLY DUG GRAVES.

Oh Jesus, she says. *No.*

SUDDEN CUT TO BLACK SCREEN.

CREDITS ROLL IN SILENCE

OVER THE GREAT NOTHING WE HEAR CHAIRS OVERTURN & GLASSES LOSE THEIR GRIP ON THE NARRATIVE. FEET STARTLE, FOLLOWED BY A STAMPEDE OF VOICES THAT BEGIN AS MURMURATION & END IN BUILDINGS COLLAPSING IN GRIEF. THERE IS A DANCING FILLED WITH SILENCE.

Maryville Celeste

SOUNDTRACK: *Crying,* K.D Laing & Roy Orbison

|| TRACKING SHOT THROUGH THE INTERRUPTED BAR, PAST THE DESERTED CHRISTMAS TABLE & ITS COUNCIL OF CHRISTMAS HATS, AROUND OVERTURNED CHAIRS & DROPPED CONVERSATIONS, ALONG A BAR WIDOWED WITH DRINKS. A LAUGH HANGS IN THE AIR UNSURE OF THIS NEW GROUND. A CONFETTI OF PULLED CRACKER JOKES FLURRIES FROM THE CEILING. A LIPSTICK RIMMED CIGARETTE BURNS IN AN ASHTRAY, ITS SMOKE FORMING THE SHAPE OF A BOI RUNNING TOWARD THE OPEN MOUTH OF GOD. MUSIC STANDS IN THE CORNER AND WILL NOT MEET OUR EYE. THE CAMERA PAUSES & LOOKS TOWARD THE GAPE OF MARYVILLE'S ENTRANCE. THE CAMERA DOES NOT WANT TO PASS THROUGH IT. IT LOOKS BACK OVER ITS SHOULDER. INSIDE THE BAR EVERYTHING WAITS, PRESERVED IN THE AMBER LIGHT. THE CAMERA TAKES A BREATH & MOVES FORWARD INTO THE AFTERWARD. ||

SLOW FADE TO CLOSE ANGLE CAMERA SHOT, GROUND LEVEL, LOOKING UP.

||POV ANGEL ||

The bois stand like nativity / looking down at the body of Angel / Vitruvian on the night pavement / worshipping her / as if she were just born / they have brought gifts: a shout in a glass / a tear drop on a tie pin / a fist in the act of becoming a butterfly / Jack watches blood emigrate to the gutter / around them / fireflies whisk colours into figures / the dark buzzes / voices blur / Jack holds Angel's hand / & Valentine holds Jack's hand / & Dudizile holds Valentine's hand / & they are all linked / like Christmas decorations in an old bar / like the lost at sea.

|| POV ANGEL: A SLOW FADE TO BLACK ||

ONCE BLACKED THE SCREEN IS PIERCED WITH A FULL STOP OF LIGHT. THE LIGHT EXPANDS & BREATHES UNTIL IT IS THE WHOLE OF THE SCREEN. WE CAN ALMOST SEE OURSELVES IN IT. CASS IS THERE, & SAM & VELDA, BEE IS THERE, WITH TERRY & RACHEL, JAMIE & AVIE. WE WALK INTO THEM. A HAND RESTS ON OUR RIGHT SHOULDER. OUR TIE CORRECTED.

CUT

(　　　　　　　　　)

MISE-EN-SCÈNE

Jack & Soho

SOUNDTRACK: *a silence folded into a top pocket.*

|| POV SOHO BEHIND THE BAR, WIDE ANGLE ||

SHALLOW FOCUS ON THE THREE REMAINING BOIS. THEY SIT STILL & BREATHLESS WHILE BEHIND THEM THE SCENE IS SPED UP X 20. POLICE VECTOR THE BAR LIKE BLUE BOTTLES, RESTING ON THE GOUGED TURKEY, THE AVALANCHE OF TRIFLE, A SLALOM OF PINT GLASSES.

THE BOIS SIT IN CONGREGATION AT THE SHRINE OF THE BAR TOP, LOOKING UP AT THE SPIRITS WHO IGNORE THEM. THEIR FACES ARE LIT IN A DIRTY RAINBOW CAST THROUGH THE STAINED-GLASS WINDOW BOTTLES AS THE SUN GETS DRESSED & THE DAY SHAKES OUT THE STAINED STREET. NO ONE WANTS TO MOVE. TO MOVE WOULD MEAN THAT THE CLOCK WILL BEGIN TO TICK AGAIN.

POV SOHO REACHES A PAINTED HAND TOWARD JACK WHO TAKES IT AS THOUGH IT IS COMMUNION. THEY WALK TOWARD THE BACK OF THE BAR & UPSTAIRS TO THEIR FLAT.

After the red turns to blue
after the street flashes at them
after officers arrest the air
after the evidence brushes itself down
after prayers are returned unopened
comes Soho
she takes Jack by the hand
to an old enamel bathtub
runs it without breaking eye contact
& bathes her
full suited brogues tightly laced
a soft-soft less of a cleansing
more of a clearing Soho makes space for Jack
again in her bod / y /
Jack weeps the bath water rises
she folds into night
& Soho washes it off her all of it
the blood the barter
prayer of police ambulance indifference
how breath runs away from the body
as if searching for its mother
the bath water chills
grits its teeth
a skin of ice heals over Jack
sleet falls like friends
until she is sculpture
the whole room
preserved in a snow globe.

|| POV SOHO: SHE RETREATS FROM THE ROOM, EYES STILL FIXED ON JACK WHO SITS SILENT & STILL, A SUBMERGED CITY REACHING THROUGH THE FROZEN FLOOD ||

CAMERA FADES SLOWLY TO BLACK AS THOUGH THE WHOLE CINEMA IS LOWERING ITS EYES.

MISE-EN-SCÈNE

Funeral for a Friend

|| EXTREME WIDE SHOT. FILMED IN BLACK & WHITE; COLOUR WAS NOT INVITED & MOURNS ALONE IN THE ALL-NIGHT CAFÉ ||

A CHURCHYARD IN EAST LONDON.

THE CEMETRY IS EMPTY. BIRDS TAKE BACK THEIR SONGS. THERE ARE NO FRIENDS OR LOVERS ATTENDING, JUST A MOTHER WHO DID NOT KNOW HOW TO SPELL HER & A FATHER WHOSE HANDS SHE TOOK WITH HER. THE COFFIN IS CLOSED. EVERTHING IS CLOSED. AS THE COFFIN IS LOWERED:

CUT AWAY SHOT: TILT SHIFT. BLACK & WHITE. INTERIOR MARYVILLE BAR.

Jack sits on the opposite side of the bar / pours a shot / & becomes it / Dudz strokes the fabric of Angel's first suit / cradles it to her breast / whispers the lullaby of unliving / Valentine shaves her head / until it becomes a crystal ball / in it she watches her boi / propelled from life / into a dark wide mouth.

|| CAMERA PANS THE BAR ||

around them / snow falls like expectation / falls & falls & falls / like television static / like binary code / & the whole of Maryville is re written.

|| ANANMORPHIC SHOT ||

a blizzard storms into the bar / without wiping its feet / it has her face / Jack can almost kiss it / snowbanks build up across the doors / drifting over the tables / & layering the dance floor / niveous / it snows & it snows / onto the old bois / a dusting across their lapels / a flurry behind spectacles / all of their hands blue.

at the windows snowmen block the light and watch with fathomless eyes.

CUT AWAY SHOT

Angel is buried in a coffin like a sealed envelope.
this is all we know.

CLOSE-UP OF A SNOWFLAKE

it is cathedral.
is there anything as beautiful as a dead boi?

EPISODE THREE, SEASON ONE

1997 – 2007

dust kings. tough kids.

MISE-EN-SCÈNE

1997-2007

SOUNDTRACK: *A Deeper Love,* Aretha Franklin & C.C Hot Mix

EXTERIOR, SIDE STREET IN LONDON, NIGHT.

|| CAMERA WALKS PAST A HOLLOW OF BOY-BOYS TOWARD THE MARYVILLE. CLOSE-UP ON SIGN. AN 'L' NO LONGER ILLUMINATES, SO IT NOW READS:

MARYVI LE

THE CAMERA PUSHES OPEN THE DOOR.

INTERIOR MARYVILLE, NIGHT

RAPID DOLLYTRACK THROUGH THE BAR PAST CROWDS OF COLOURS & CHATTERING GLIMMER. THE CAMERA RACES TOWARD THE BAR TOP AND FOCUSES ON JACK CATCH BEHIND IT POLISHING SNOWGLOBES. IN ONE IS AN UNUSED WRAP OF AMPHETAMINE & IN ANOTHER, A LOCK OF ANGEL'S FIST. JACK IS WEARING HER HOUNDSTOOTH SUIT WITHOUT THE JACKET, HER SLEEVES HELD UP BY STAINLESS STEEL BRACES. HER HAIR IS THE WHITE OF BAD NEWS, HER FACE UNDERLINED LIKE A RESEARCH PAPER ||

POV JACK CATCH:

Soho reclines at the end of the bar / atemporal / held together with sellotape & bad jokes / a halo of smoke resting above her head / a portrait in the attic / young bois lay shivers at her feet / & learn the importance of speed / Jack winks / & it becomes a bird that rests on her shoulder / Dudz leans against the wall to the toilets / straightening collars / unbuttoning waistcoats / frisking the tie / while Valentine revs up a wild story / one about lesbian communes / lipstick on walls / the dildo wars of 94 / talking about anything / other than the thing that must be talked about / & around them / a revolving door of faces flicker & mute / a microfiche of the decade / until it stills / releasing the bois like sad greyhounds / into the bar / each of them / staring into their hands / as if they hold thrilling eggs / & Jack wonders / how anyone can tell these days / where a story ends / & an evening begins / one by one / the regulars blur & sputter / & are sucked into their phones / face first / until the only real thing / is the thing that is not there.

LIGHTS STUTTER & SETTLE. THE BAR CHANGES: ITS ROUGH OUTLINE RENDERED IN PIXELS, ITS TOILET A CHAT ROOM – UNTIL IT SLOWLY TRANSFORMS INTO AN ONLINE SPACE. THE MODERATOR HAS LEFT THE ROOM, THE DOOR SWINGING.

Coin Slot

1997 / your cunt a coin slot / in the erotic arcade / the shiver & clench / of feminist rough trade / putting the gay into game / your cunt is Pac Man / eating the road it hovers above / & you are alive again / bigger than your body / this new knowing / you squat your heart / change the locks, re-wire / stand in circles & snort your own face / the photographs on cigarette packets / rarely show the glamorous side of addiction / but you are it / gloss lipped & dingy / a magic brutalism / postmodern post fucking / the high cost of rimming / less free love / more hepatitis b / & you are making your own porn / but the stars / are your friends / you write scenes you are afraid to watch / you write scenes but rack up your lines / it is a seamless transition / from chaining yourself to fences / to chaining yourself to bed posts / putting the suffering into suffrage / & suddenly Jack is not sure / who the villain / & who Verlaine / it's all so fin-de-psycho / young things wear their dark on their sleeves / trade mark 'anxiety'/ patent pending / mental health as accessory / & everything matches / everyone is equal / it is the only bigotry / the free meat market / kiss one get two free / but in the panorama of sexual drama / things are looking messy on the mesa level / jealousy has not read the instruction manual / she says / she will tell you what she wants / what she really *really* wants / but never does / but its ok / relax / you are the young things / handsome & tingling / stood beside one another bandaged in leather / she says, you look like a boy band / *No Life* / & suddenly you are mounted / on revolving bar stool pedestals / soon you will stand up / & walk into the camera.

SOHO

Vespertine

SCENE FADES UP ON A THREAD OF CIGARETTE SMOKE THAT HOOKS THE CAMERA & PULLS IT INEXORABLY TOWARD SOHO, STILL HERE, STILL EXTRAVAGENTLY MINIMAL. BEHIND HER WE CAN SEE JACK CATCH'S SILHOUETTE POLISHING SNOWGLOBES.

dressed as a three-card trick
    her gown a magician's handkerchief

        revealing in a flourish a pink rabbit
            which strips down to the knot of a girl

            an ingenue in somber, vespertine lady
                only flowering at night, a shriek

in an ombre dress o sad siren
    we search the skies above the dance floor

        for a sign, omen, the birds
            are emptying their suitcases across us

        the dogs have rented condos
            Soho is the disappearing woman

there & not there
    a chair you were sure
        someone once sat in.

THE BOIS

Halo

|| RACK SHOT TO THE THREE REMAINING BOIS. OLDER NOW; ANOTHER DECADE RIDDEN BAREBACK ACROSS THEIR BROWS ||

the old bois / are grey fur & fuck you / their teeth ungentrified / the gaps between / the spaces in conversation / their skies derelict / all the gods in early retirement / they speak of Angel as though she still breathes / beyond the window, mythic / perfectly imperfect / absurd legend / woman as sacrament / never more alive / than when she died.

JACK CONTINUES TO POUR A PINT FOR ANGEL.

IT SITS ON THE BAR TOP LIKE A CENOTAPH.

THE CIRCLE IT LEAVES IS A HALO.

DUDIZILE

Quipu

a slow night
at the Maryville
a display case
of businessmen's
tongues open
on the bar
as if the rainbow
has been skinned
she is tutoring
the rare young
the undercooked
& unfinished
how to fasten a tie
what each knot means
what it remembers
like the Inca used knots
to tell a story
she will teach
the fatherless daughters
this is the Four in Hand
& this the Half Windsor
the Tulip, the Balthus
Murrell & this one
this is the day you knew
& this the year of forgetting
this the lie
this the revelation

the curdling town
the flocks of fists
that feed from your hand
each small seed
a reversing family
& here is the day you
understood
that a suit is a map
an escape tunnel
that leads to here
right here
how beautiful is a boi's tear
a crystal tip on a tie pin
she stands behind
arms around the boi
& together
they coax the knot.

SOHO

The Femme Telegraph

BUTCHES & FEMMES DRESSED AS ARRIVAL COLONISE THE TABLES, THE BUTCHES SEARCHING FOR THEMSELVES IN THE PALMS OF THEIR SILVERY HANDS, WHILE THE FEMMES ARTICULATE AIR, BEND IT INTO AN IMPLEMENT THEY MIGHT USE TO PRY OPEN THE BOIS, WHO GATHER LIKE LOCKED SAFES IN THE BOTTOM OF CANALS.

across the swollen bar / femmes flick their fingers / an air braille / (a fetish sign language) / each of their fingers / telling a different story / the index finger for the bad butch that did it / the third finger / bowing slightly / is her / the other fingers / are bar drift / a parent perhaps / & they signal their intimate epics / across to each other / tear a page off the day / reply / enact a murder / each of their hands / ballerinas with machetes / making shadow puppets / that loom over the heads / of the congregation / spreading across the walls like colonisers / like a weather report / & now / they are bringing in the big puppets / full hands / this is ancient television / & Jack flinches when she sees / the shadows become east end lions / skinny with truth / & desperate to suck / it is clear there has been a wrong / doing / here this night / she bows a shaven head / polishes a glass / until her reflection is rubbed out.

MISE-EN-SCÈNE

Everyone is Still Alive

SOUNDTRACK: *Love & Affection,* Joan Armatrading

INTERIOR MARYVILLE, EARLY HOURS. A SILENCE WE CAN CUT A PATTERN FROM. ALL THE GHOSTS ARE RETURNING. THE CAMERA RESTS IN A SNOW GLOBE & WATCHES.

on the stage
a drag queen is peeling

down to the pith of a boy
who strips to the seed of a first kiss

light bankrupts the bathroom
as a woman high kicks out of her cunt

the drapes smacking their lips
behind her to the roar of closet doors

the bar serves pints of belief
that drip down our pink gingham shirts

we Ben Sherman she men
we bull footed women

shoals of old bois in herringbone
pilot the bar, bioluminescent

brave as bank holidays
leading us to safer waters

a way out of the net.

& the dance floor
is a collapsed lung

a hole healed
in the chest of a boi

her smile a blue and white cordon
around a loud body.

THE VOLUME OF THE SOUNDTRACK RISES UNTIL IT BECOMES A WHITE NOISE, A SNOW FALLING ACROSS ALL OF US ACROSS TIME. THROUGH THE BLIZZARD WE CAN SEE THE SHAPE OF WHAT IS TO COME. CAMERA FADES & FORGETS ITS HISTORY, ITS BATTLES & BECOMINGS, ITS COMMUNALITY & ITS VIBRANT NO.

THE BOIS

The O God

// from this distance / church bells look like bombs dropping / o lord the sky has broken / into middle aged men / there she is / bruised to rainbow bunting / how was she to know that / to light a cigarette was to light a fuse / her face / white against the sudden / behind her / buildings falling to their knees / birds taking back their songs / all this little black / how hello can be the end of the world / how you can fall into its o / where did I put my shoes? / is there a reason for a coat? / o lord the butches are climbing inside each other / chasing down ghosts / diving from high rises into the bodies of swans / that frisk the air / correct the parting / the tie tightening / o lord I'm moving into the horror of my heart / combing my hair / making appointments / searching for a wall to line books against / a view to somewhere that isn't me / mine's a pint of father, please / I want a mirror that shows me where I went wrong / here's me pulling apart the bird / to find the source of the song //

MISE-EN-SCÈNE

Snowglobes

SOUNDTRACK: *Glad to be Gay,* Tom Robinson

INTERIOR, NIGHT, MARYVILLE BAR

DOLLY CAMERA EDGES INTO THE MAIN SPACE & LISTENS. IT IS LONG PAST CLOSING & THE BAR IS REMEMBERING ITSELF. BEHIND THE COUNTER IS A CHOIR OF SNOWGLOBES, EACH CRADLING ITS OWN SONG. AS WE WATCH THE SNOWGLOBES THEY BEGIN TO PULSE WITH A SOFT LIGHT. THE SNOWGLOBES SEMAPHORE ACROSS THE ROOM, EACH A GLOWING COSMOS, A CHARM ON A BRACELET. INSIDE EACH GLOBE IS ANOTHER BAR IN ANOTHER CITY ACROSS THE WORLD. IF WE WERE TO LOOK INTO ONE, WE MIGHT FIND OURSELVES STARING BACK, A HAND AGAINST THE GLASS, MOUTHING AN OLD SHOW TUNE.

THE SNOWGLOBES FLARE AMBER & WRITE ON THE DARK CLOTH OF EARLY MORNING:

all of the ghosts. all of them.

after closing / in the dim light of the one arm bandit / a nimbus of cigarette smoke waits against the ceiling / made of last breaths, it is patient / seeking a tear in the silence / some tacky air to grip to / on the hour / the penumbra slowly unfolds / uncoils from Artex / & swoons to the floor / each tendril unwrapping into an arm/ a torso / the profile of a face / all of the ghosts returning / (everyone is still alive in the land of the dead) / o this is a summoning / this is a riot / a woman grows from a wound / the centre of her chest an event horizon / & other women clamber through / dazed in their abandoned bodies / in the amber bar / ancient insects / remembering geometry / here come the old ones / the mollies & jacks / cheap quintrelles & filthy dappers / cervical monocles / handkerchiefs dropping like bread crumbs / carnations flowering into green flames / hands passing straight through ideas / & now the young ones come / watermarks against the air / born into the bar / *I was almost home* / *I walked too close to my girlfriend* / *my face has never liked me* / & all move their diaphanous symphony / silver & thinking / toward the snow globes behind the bar / which brighten at their approach / a light left on in the hallway / & through it all / the silhouette of Soho / smoking in her usual seat / as though cigarettes were penance.

THE CAMERA STAYS UP LATE & SITS QUIETLY WATCHING THE CINEMA OF SNOWGLOBES. IT MOVES CLOSER TO INVESTIGATE ONE, STEPPING THROUGH ITS GLASS WALL.

dust kings. tough kids

(i)

for bois slow dancing in snow globes
moored in suits stitched from rainfall
who hold each other like eggs
from which they will hatch, punch-
curious, alert to the wild
as snow falls like empires;
grass grows though the dance
floor, & the bois are night butterflies.
everything cracks in the end.
but not this hand. this idea.
some nights it snows spare change
or saliva, handkerchiefs, or charge sheets.

dust kings & tough kids
we had nothing. & we shared it

(ii)

we had nothing. & we shared it
a neat division of air, woke spinning
on bar stools, or crawling from hedgerows,
naked. we took these skins from shop windows
saville row, paris, bangkok
we were trying to remember why we died.
or if there was a sound. if the birds
forgot the words to their songs
or if the sky called our mothers.
we were trying to remember if we were special.
we keep saying goodnight
but we can't remember who to.

we are reborn in the bar beneath the city
each of us haunting the halls of our bodies

(iii)

we were haunting the halls of our bodies
long before we were squeezed from our skins
we were ghosts of school linoleum
ghosts of the changing room
ghosts of the long walk home
the board room the ballot box
ghosts of our mouths
we were watercolours in rainfall
dissolving on the streets, the back seats of buses
erased, invisible, a taste, heavy air
when & how we died unnoticed:
how do you kill something that isn't there?

but we were sacred before we surrendered
this much each of us remembers

(iv)

what each of us remembers
comes as snow in the globe
gold binary code, it comes fractal.
we hold the memory, & it sobs:
george returns leaning over the pool table
the balls escaping their pockets
my head, she says, & we look
through a hole in her skull
toward her last moments:
the breath. the blue. violent circus
that chased her out of her skin.
here we rise headfirst from pint glasses

or materialise in ironic lines for the Ladies
each nursing a wound, a violet baby

(v)

we each nursed a wound, a violate baby: la
camionera, machorra, unravels a bruise
like a blueprint, a map of her final route
the topography of body, when we lean
close we see the fist-swarm who followed
from the bar as though tied by strings
to her waist, umbilical somehow, a leash, a howl,
dog men drawn by the scent of dissidence
of independence, of stubborn (she didn't mean it,
any of it, shirts are just shirts, shaved hair returns
like evening tide) but the night hung limp
in their jaws, punctured into heavenly bodies.

she rolled a cigarette, smiled when they caught her
(red in water), all hail the non-conformist daughter

(vi)

(red in water). all hail the non-conformist daughter
all hail ugly. all hail disobedient
& women who identify as freedom &
justice, as hope for fuck's sake, in the face
of those who would bury the rainbow.
a clutter of jackrolling boys took her
translating kisses into curses, fear
into prophecy, their pornographic grins
a woman splayed, red curtains parting, dark entertainment.
when jackrolling smiles connect, they make a red lit lane
leading to a flick of blue light somewhere south of here
it's a bonding, a ritual, cocks held like crucifixes:

(they would have left her if she had begged forgiveness)
a woman's body is always a man's business

(vii)

A woman's body is a man's business
wet currency, his penis a monument
erected to himself, I understand now
that language can eat us, that the mirror
is carniverous, that when we cut
our hair it doesn't stop bleeding
that when we are dressing, we mean
as if over a wound, please understand
we are trying to tame our own faces
so they come when they are called
these small uprisings, these last stands
a knuckle of butches backed against gender

some women's bodies are the site of their protest
some women are buried in the graves between their legs

(viii)

some of us are buried in the graves between
our legs. we open them like books, & the past
falls out, fully formed, bloodied, blinking.
 our mothers fall out, clutching
the hands of their mothers, until the whole
paper chain of women, arms
linked like chromosomes, is pulled
into the sun & in this way we inherit each other's
grief, which is a kind of a coat, is a kind
woman nodding silently across the bus seats,
a word returned to its birthplace, a silent knowing
is a language that teaches the tongue to be still

we inherit one another which is a kind of a warning
all of us women trapped inside the bodies of women

(ix)

we were women trapped inside the bodies
of women, until we were not, & then
we flew, out of the car, between the window slit,
from behind the skip, from shallow burials &
disco funerals, we rose and remembered
& returned, back to the bar, back to what the skin
had learned, we gathered like smoke, & loved.
Dudz completed her shot
Angel inhaled the line around her body
 & Jack lifted her pint glass to the light
& we were all there, caught in its amber.

pulled through the earth, birthed back to the beginning
looking through the holes in us to who we might have been

(x)

we were looking through the holes in us
to who we might have been; how
were we to know the weight of a hole,
how heavy it is, how bright, how egg?
what might be born from this wound
what face might find me, what ordinary
happy? i might have been a woman
who makes dinner, or mistakes, or the bed
she will be buried in, a quiet woman
in a loud body, i might have lived
like a river running uphill, but here
we turn from the cinemas at the centre of us

afraid of ourselves, our seditious genetics
examining our faces as though they are relics

(xi)

examine our faces as though they are relics:
noxola xakeke, sizakele siqasa, salome masooa,
simanagele nhalpo, crystal turner madoe
mafubedu, zoliswa nkonyana, eudy simelane,
marielle franco, fanny ann eddy, luana barbosa
dos reis santos, yelena grigoryeva,
kylen schulte, roxanne ellis, michelle abdill, monica
biones, mariapia castro, nicole saavedra
bahamondes, anna crook, rebecca wright, mollie
olgen, susana sanhueza, carolina torres, cynthia
leslie velasquez, elisa pomarelli, bonang galeae
sisanda gumede, lima katso puling, sakia gunn

the glamour of the dead. here we are proud
draped in suits as if they were shrouds

(xii)

draped in suits like shrouds, we returned,
three-pieces sewn in bone and belonging,
hemlined in headlines, threaded in chromosomes.
a cravat bleeds. white cotton clenches.
note the wire fences woven into the fabric, grave
markers. a suit is an inheritance:
we hold on to the end of red thread –
bull dykes lost in the labyrinth –
& pull, our faces blunt instruments.
remember the running stitch, sister? the catch stitch. chain.
we are sutured in suits, our lineage a lemniscate skein,
remind me again, what is the healing time of a stitch?

these suits on girls. armour, mother, womb
see how everything changes in the changing room?

(xiii)

everything changes in the changing room:
we strip down to the kernels of girls
with men's faces, bury our breasts for the dogs,
newton's cradle chest, bulls lassoed by bra
straps, by mathematics. we float out
of our uniforms, a pale steam haunt,
as cherry blossom ejaculates from shower heads.
it is here we all learn to fight.
that fighting is backward kissing.
that all fists return to their source:
i once planted a fist in a boy & it flowered.
i wear it pinned to my lapel, a bruise lavender.

but look at us now – bois– lined up like snooker balls
o tonight – bois – the stars are glory holes

(xiv)

tonight, bois, the stars are glory holes:
this is not a safe space, but it is brave:
we knit the edges of the dance floor
(after all that, we eroticised survival)
dressed in exits, municipal leather,
council flat tweed, twill, denim, a shaven image.
handkerchiefs semaphore from ripped jeans
pockets wink, steel zips lick their lips, lapels flutter
& lay their gifts on the ground. we
are water in the act of drinking itself.
this is not a brave space, but it is ecstatic
our bodies hypothetical, thought experiments

we have risen from the dead to reclaim our fucking
schrödinger's daughters. tough kids. dust kings.

(xv) *crown*

dust kings. tough kids. we had nothing. & we shared it.
haunting the halls of our bodies
this much each of us remembers
nursing a wound, a violate baby
(red in water) all hail the non-conformist daughter.
a woman's body is always a man's business
but some women are buried in the graves between their legs
some women are trapped inside the bodies of women
looking through the holes in us to who we might have been
examining our faces as though they are relics
draped in suits like shrouds –
but everything changes in the changing room:

o tonight, bois, the stars are glory holes
& in every snowglobe a falling Angel

THE CAMERA BACKS SOFTLY OUT OF THE FINAL GLOBE & RETURNS TO ITS SEAT. WE CAN HEAR FOOTSTEPS ON THE STAIRS DRAGGING THE DAY TO ITS FEET. THE FRONT DOOR SLAMS.

JACK CATCH

Old Jack Takes a Long Walk Back to the Beginning

This day // the sun is a circle left by a pint glass // & the Shard is a femme's raised middle finger // its shadow turns the city into a sundial // which sweeps time into the gutter // where it belongs // Jack walks through its tick // & years fall from her face // like drunks from barstools // wrinkles unravel into red carpets // that lead into the past // five decades unroll // the lines at the corner of her eyes // hands on a clock purring // Jack keeps walking // Morse of her Blakey's // a message she has tried so long not to send // but here we are again // 16 & sickened by love // incarcerated in a confession box heart // visited by a girl in Sunday School // who in that vast dusk sees Jack // who becomes solid beneath her thinking // & there is something about hands // the way they leave the body // & return with glitter & furrow // learn to hold a secret like a bluebottle in a fist // to live in the held breath // learn the tyranny of love // see how shame is a chaperone // that buzzes & breeds // sits beside them on the church bench // sleeps between them in their rough bed // the dark tunnel where they learned to see // it is the sudden opening of a door // that locks Jack behind another // a father black as priests // a lover murdering courage // & an evangelical Jack // who believed in love // until it came for her // perhaps our first loves are always our first deaths // Jack touches the sting where her heart hid // betrayal is a girl with eyes like the tunnels they kissed in // a dead girl in lipstick // a child thrown overboard to save the ship // a dust mother who disperses // a daughter discarded // Jack sighs // this is how it was // but even now // she carries that shame like a gold censer // her confessional box

// rocking with ignored truths // o Old Jack // sad Jack // you should know by now // you can let go of her hand // but you will never stop holding it. //

OLD BOIS

2007

(i)

Valentine

Valentine
is dressed
in mutter
gaberdine slacks
an open white
shirt, parted
to reveal a neck
like an oil rag
twisted & hash
tagged, a dirty
strength
She picks up
her pint
but it veers
from her mouth
an accelerator
accidently clipped
a swerve, then
this oil slick of lager
across the clean
white in the shape
of a country
she has never visited

maybe she needs
a road trip an
action movie
she examines
her veins raised
like motorway
bridges, under
pass, her skin
an unmanaged
side street, the kind
of carriageway
that might tear
if it got wet
when femmes see
her it is with
gentleness, a cruel
sad, her smile a skid
& Valentine knows
she is almost
out of road
it is almost time
before the rains
almost time
to go home.

(ii)

Dudizile

Dudizile holds herself
up between the counter
& a stool, a bewildered
soldier walking
across the battlefield
toward the light
of women laughing.
Precision dressing.
A trilby gifted & tilted
pocket square:
a brown envelope
snapping socks
a tie that talks
behind her back
she is considering
the reflection
in her rum
how the years
have pulled
at her face
until it is a
stretched muslin
she won't be able
to make anything
useful out of.
She coughs.
Grey grief climbs
her scalp

her legs have
almost stopped
running
cannot catch
her now
she is almost
home.

(iii)

Jack Catch

Jack polishes
the glasses
the globes
her face
her customers
the air
as though
she is rubbing
them out
quietly erasing
five decades
polishing Elizabeth
& the boy-boys
the prison
how liberation
does not mean freedom
polishing the night
Angel fell
into Heaven
polishing the tick
the rub, each laugh
& sideways smile
polishing everything
but Soho
who does not wish
to be clean
likes to read
the fingerprints

mapping her body
& Jack wonders
how Soho
never ages
just leans slightly
more into her face
polishes & marvels
how a woman
this woman
can be the shape
 of a home.

//

Outside
the boy-boys' lips
are thin trumpets
heralding a young
butch, their voices
tearing the night
in two, a wound.

Behind the bar
snow globes
frisk & whinny.

COWBOY SHOT OF THE OLD BOIS STARING TOWARD THE SALOON DOORS. A YOUNG BOI STUMBLES IN BRUSHING SILENCE FROM HER SHOULDERS, HER EYES DARK CIRCUSES. THE OLD BOIS STAND STRAIGHT. THE CAMERA REALISES THEIR INTENTION, & RETREATS TO A SAFE DISTANCE.

Prelude

When the three old bois walk to the door
Angel's shadow unpeels from the wall & joins them

each old boi an unbuttoning blazer
simplifying the tie, wrapping their belts

around their startled fists.
They sadwink to a flock of femmes

who stand, each of their faces deserted cinemas.
Soho closes her eyes: it is now, she thinks, Jesus

it is always now. It always will be
four abreast, chests like newly made beds

All these years walking past, tipping their hats
letting insults roll off them like lovers

Maryville is hushed now, inevitable
young bois bow to the silverbacks

offer to lend them their spit, their teeth
but the old bois have everything they need

50 winters deep, a friendship tight as coins in a sock
wearing each other's smiles as knuckle dusters

Youngs dressed in a different language nod
their eyes low windows left unlocked

that the old bois would guard all night
like they patrol this small place of being

they sigh in synchronicity, shake out their shoulders
like beloved library rugs, let the dust rise

find form, idea, & walk with them too
a ghost reprise for this slow dance

How can we live within parenthesis?

What is space if not a filling?

Each knowing their final breaths will become
another four butches' first inhale into body

At the door they pause for a moment
in which four lifetimes are lived

They look back at the bar, at Soho
 at the clean & the offcuts

the swoons & the thugs
the cock sure & cock shy

butches with comfort blankets
femmes with socket wrenches

how everything is something else
the quantum physics of fucking

a door that will open into closure
where a monolith of boy-boys stand

guarding the entrance from themselves
Moai now, almost ritual, corner gods

The Old Bois shrug
& pass each other a look

like a note between desks.
then walk through the door.

|| CAMERA AIMED DIRECTLY INTO
THE FACE OF THE READER ||

The Door

On the other side of the door
is Jack's father
he is opening his arms
& releasing a small girl
who bursts into a bright
murmuration of starlings.

                              On the other side of the door
                              are Valentine's brothers
                              smelling of oil & Old Spice
                              smiles eating their faces
                              they hand her a bouquet of
                              wrenches she keeps in a vase.

On the other side of the door
is an immigration official
who checks Dudizile's passport
her visa, asylum status
but won't let her into
her body, that strange country.

'The world was ending & it was time to dance.' Derek Jarman

THE CAMERA HUNCHES IN THE CENTRE OF A CIRCLE
OF OLD BOIS & BOY-BOYS, SWINGING TO FOLLOW THE
ARC OF EACH PUNCH, THE BRIGHT RED BREATH OF
LEAVING.

Old Jack / body like ash falling from a cigarette / more powder than breath / more bone than think / spits in the grin of the boy-boys / who curl & snicker / Valentine is in shape / (just the wrong one) / she laughs / & it is the sound of a Harley / leaving the road / becoming bird becoming comet / she throws a punch like an arm around a girl / while Jack buries a hand deep into a soft belly / as though it is pregnant with Angel / O Angel / & she might pull her out again / Dudizile stands / a suit on a hanger / unoccupied / thrown back to the long run / her hands sprinters crouched at a start line / her breath still ahead of her / all these years / & she still hasn't caught it / she remembers her legs / & kicks bright red confetti / into the evening air / the men in front of them / have aged as they have / faded like Maryville's paint work / bellies become shopping bags in the rain / their chests stiffened into Artex / their nicotine skin / at the window Soho watches / through hyphenated eyes / the whole bar crowded around her / the living & the dead / & still they fight / like women drowning / like sad fish in a bucket / (is life worth dying for?) / (this parenthesis?) / when the men hit back / it is with all of their wanting / each fist clutching / a bouquet of supermarket roses / exploding into dank petals / that spread like rumours across the Old Bois / Jack is still fighting / long after she dies / her face / split cinema / while Valentine's stag heart / leaps into the dark /

grabbing her into a last kiss / before the lights come up / & from the window / it all looks like ballet / & maybe that's where Dudz thinks she is / maybe this no man's land is a ballroom / perhaps this is a waltz / & though she is not sure which one of them is leading / she dances until the stars dilate / into three white tunnels / marvelling / as cherry blossom grows from their touch / & blood runs / like a frightened child / there is no honour in this final hour / just this immovable friendship / this loss / this terrible expanse of love.

Homecoming

The old bois
are tangled
thinking
red proof
marks correcting
the pavement
Snow falls
from the lit
end of Soho's
cigarette
She pulls
flocked wall
paper tighter
to her chest
turns
& sinks
into the floor
The windows
look at their feet
the jukebox
takes back
music
lager returns
to the tap
& the lights
of Maryville
wave their
wise retreat
blinking

its binary
into
his
story
into
fu
ll
st
op
.

MISE-EN-SCÈNE

O Maryville O

INTERIOR, MARYVILLE, DEEP EVENING. THE BAR IS EMPTY OF ALL BUT ITS IDEAS.

THE CAMERA SWEEPS THE CHAIRS & AS IT LOOKS AT THEM, THEY FILL. THE DUSTY MIRRORBALL THROWS GHOSTS ACROSS THE WALL.

A PUMP BEGINS ITS IMPOTENT ARC TOWARD AN INVISIBLE GLASS WHICH FILLS WITH EVERYTHING YOU HAVE LOST. FOUR PEDESTALS BEFORE THE BAR TOP GENTLY SPIN & SLOWLY DRAW THEMSELVES IN: AN ARM, A QUIFF, THE MINNOW OF A SMILE DARTING TO COVE. THERE IS THE SMELL OF DAMP TWEED. A LAUGH HANGS IN THE AIR & VALENTINE SWINGS FROM IT. A COMB IS DRAWN FROM A POCKET & AS IT WORKS DUDIZILE'S HEAD APPEARS, YOUNG & SHINING.

THE DARK IS ALIVE. THE CEILING IS A GLASS DOME & SNOW IS PULLED UPWARD TOWARD IT LIKE WOMEN CLIMBING ROPES TO HEAVEN.

AN UNLIT CIGARETTE MATERIALISES IN THE CENTRE OF THE SCREEN. THERE IS A BOREDOM & EXACTNESS THAT WHITTLES THE SILENCE INTO LONG FINGERNAILS.

THE VOICE WHEN IT ARRIVES IS A MURMURATION OF STARLINGS:

Hey

Hey Jack

Got a light?

A ZIPPO UNZIPS THE NIGHT.

|| GRADUAL FADE TO BLACK ||

End Notes

[i] *Cahalane, Claudia, "Lip Service is groundbreaking – whatever its star says" The Guardian (13 October 2010).*

[ii] (stopvaw/prevalence_6)

[iii] (Sddirect.org/blog-article/violence-against-lgbtqi-people-hidden-pandemic).

[iv] (Stopvaw.org/violence-against-women).

[v] https://www.hrw.org/report/2023/02/14/why-we-became-activists/violence-against-lesbian-bisexual-and-queer-women-and-non

[vi] Judge Eric Pickles in the trial of Jennifer Saunders in 1991, a 17-year old who was sentenced to six years for sex by deception. Her two girlfriends alleged they did not know she was female.

[vii] South Africa slang: to force (a lesbian) into sex with multiple men; a form of gang rape.

[viii] The Strip: a term used for inmates of Holloway Prison who were sent to solitary confinement. There is an irony here.

[ix] During the 1970s increasing numbers of London properties were abandoned and reclaimed by lesbian squatters. It is thought that London Fields in East London had over 50 squatted lesbian communes while even more were founded across Hackney and Brixton.

[x] Clause 28, also known as Section 28 of the Local Government Act 1988, was a law that prohibited local authorities in the UK from promoting homosexuality

[xi] The London Lesbian and Gay Centre was a lesbian and gay community centre located at 67–69 Cowcross Street, London. It was established in 1985 by the Greater London Council.

[xii] Graffiti found in Brixton, 1978 https://www.brixtonbuzz.com/2018/05/brixton-graffiti-from-the-late-1970s- and-early-1980s

[xiii] Attributed to Paul Grady aka Lily Savage in the early 1980's during a raid on the Royal Vauxhall Tavern, London.

[xiv] The 1985 Brixton Riots were sparked by the shooting of Dorothy "Cherry" Groce by the Metropolitan Police, while they sought her 21-year-old son Michael Groce in relation to a robbery and suspected firearms offence; they believed Michael Groce was hiding in his mother's home. The Brixton community reacted in protests against a racist police force that targeted young black men in particular. The police reacted with riot shields and truncheons, the protests becoming became street battles, leading to widespread uprising, disorder, and injury while buildings and cars were set on fire.

Glossary of LGBT Slang

Butch	a masculine presenting lesbian
Stud	a black masculine presenting lesbian
Boi	a young masculine presenting lesbian
Femme	lesbian presenting a heightened version of femininity
Silverback	an older butch
Boy-boys	men
Stone	a butch who prefers to touch rather than be touched
Bull	very butch lesbian
Camionera	LatinX butch
Machorra	Dyke, slur

Film Vocabulary

Establishing Shot	Initial shot that sets the scene
Extreme wide shot	Subject and environment together
Wide Shot	Focus on subject with some environment
Medium Shot	Subject from knees up
Close-Up	Whole Face
Choker Shot	Eyebrow to Mouth
Extreme Close-Up	Detail of person or scene
Cowboy Shot	From the waist up
Establishing Shot	Long shot, setting the scene
POV	Scene from POV of character
OTS	Over the shoulder of a character
Reverse Angle Shot	180 degree opposite previous shot
Focus Pull	focus lens to keep subject in view
Rack Focus	Focus shifted aggressively between subjects
Tilt Shift	Parts of image blurred
Shallow Focus	Background is blurred
Arial Shot	High above
High Angle	Looking down on subject
Cut Away Shot	Cut away from main action
Locked Down Shot	Action continues off screen
Library Shot	Prexisting film from archives
Birds Eye View	Looking down at action
Zoom	In & Out
Pan	Side to Side sequence of events
Dolly Shot	Moves on tracks
Tracking Shot	Follows subject
Ananmorphic	Everything in wide screen

Cultural References 1957 – 2007

LGBT & Women's Rights
United Kingdom & US

1957   The Wolfenden Report issued, recommending the decriminalisation of homosexuality in private between two people of the same sex.

1961   Birth control on the NHS is approved for married women (UK).

1963   Arena 3 magazine published, the UK's first lesbian publication, is published by The Minorities Research Group.

1964   The first *ladies bank* branch opened in Scotland.

1965   The first lesbians recorded in a documentary are shown on British television.

1967   The Abortion Act passed – allowing for the legalisation of abortion.

1967   The Sexual Offences Bill passed with the decriminalisation of homosexuality (UK)

1969   Stonewall Riots (US) beginning in the Stonewall Inn, Christopher Street US the riots galvanised a generation into the modern LGBT movement.

1970   The Gay Liberation Front was founded in London, UK.

1971   The first women's refuge was founded in Chiswick by Erin Pizzey.

1972   The first SPARE RIB feminist magazine is published, sparking a revolution among women.

1974   Women's Aid founded.

1975   The Sex Discrimination Act (UK) passed making dis crimination against women in the workplace illegal.
Mid 1970's to the end of 1980's lesbian squats, many on the same street, start to appear across London, notably in Hackney (East London) & Brixton (South London).

1977	Formalisation by UN of International Women's Day.
1979	Gay's the Word Lesbian & Gay bookshop established in Central London.
1981	Greenham Common Peace Camp founded, a women-only peace camp founded by Welsh nuns which protested the presence of US nuclear cruise missiles, & accidentally became a breeding ground for lesbianism & lesbian activism.
1981	First Lesbian Strength March in London.
1981	The Black Lesbian & Gay Centre established.
1981	The first case of AIDS recorded in the UK.
1982	The butches queue up to give blood to their brothers in a time when people were afraid to touch people with AIDS.
1982	Bars & clubs were no longer allowed to ban women based on their sex
1984	The London Lesbian & Gay Centre founded in Farringdon, London.
1984	Silver Moon Bookshop (feminist literature) opened on Charing Cross Road, London. 1984 – Gay's the Word Bookshop was raided by Customs & Excise who seize 140 books.
1987	AIDS Coalition to Unleash Power (ACT UP) founded in the US.
1988	Section 28 was passed into law (UK) (repealed 2003) banning the positive promotion of homosexuality as a 'pretended family unit'. This leads to a total censorship of LGBT issues in education, the arts, local government & beyond.
1988	A group of lesbian activists break into BBC News at 6pm, hosted by Sue Lawley & Nicholas Witchell, to protest Section 28.
1988	A group of activist lesbians abseil into the House of Lords to protest Section 28.1989 – Stonewall founded to oppose Section 28 and fight for gay marriage.

1989-1994 Out on Tuesday series broadcast on Channel 4, the first queer focused television series in the UK.
1990 OutRage founded, an organisation formed in response to homophobic assaults on & murders of gay men.
1994 The London Lesbian Avengers was founded by ex-Out Rage members to tackle homophobia toward lesbians directly.
1995 Dyke TV series broadcast on Channel 4.
1999 The LGBT bar The Admiral Duncan on Old Compton Street in Soho, London, bombed in a homophobic attack.
2005 Civil Partnerships established in the UK allowing same sex couples the right to legally commit to one another.

Acknowledgements

When I began to think about writing a poetry collection as a television series the dyke artist Emily Witham was my first confidante. Emily was at the start of every conversation, every image in this book. It is a unique experience to have someone who supports my art like Emily does, and I hope this book honours our thousand conversations on the subject, and her bright dissidence shines throughout.

To work with Kayo Chingonyi on evolving these poems from the back of an envelope to a full book has invigorated my thinking around what a poem wants, and what it can do. You are a joy to work with. Thanks also to the whole team at Bloomsbury.

Thanks also to my literary Laura MacDougall who has been an amazing advocate for my work, and has curated an astonishing list of LGBT authors. Thanks also to all the agents at United Agents, especially to Olivia, Eleanor and Jenny. Equal thanks to my friend and producer Tom MacAndrew, a source of infinite good advice and the best collaborator I could ask for.

Huge love & thanks to my literary collaborators at Out-Spoken for keeping me thinking & marvelling.

Rachel Smith, archivist at the Bishopsgate Institute, which holds a vast reference library of materials relating to LGBT culture, has been of invaluable help. As well as allowing access to some of the works Rachel was a vital early reader of this collection, holding the poetry against history and much more. Huge thanks also to Fisch who granted access to her extensive archive of 1980's-2000's dyke culture and helped shape the world of this book.

This book is dedicated to all the club nights across the UK that centre dykes, notably Butch, Please! – and to all the club promoters who work relentlessly to create spaces that are parenthesis, places where we find ourselves in each other's faces.

Finally, I will give the last words to the people who gave me my first words: to Mel, Ali & Fay – and Cass, of course. Always Cass.

In Memoriam
Cassandra George Johnson
Toni Macaroni
Avi Cummings
Velda Lauder
Sam Sylvan
Bee Gittens
Rachel Penny
Jamie Wildman
Terry O'Leary

A Note on the Author

TK

A Note on the Type

Warnock is a serif typeface designed by Robert Slimbach. The design features sharp, wedge-shaped serifs. The typeface is named after John Warnock, one of the co-founders of Adobe. John Warnock's son, Chris Warnock, requested that Slimbach design the typeface as a tribute to his father in 1997. It was later released as a commercial font by Adobe in 2000 under the name Warnock Pro.

MORE FROM BLOOMSBURY POETRY

TK